Collateral Damage

Culture and Politics Series

General Editor, Henry A. Giroux, Pennsylvania State University

Collateral Damage

Corporatizing Public Schools— A Threat to Democracy

Kenneth J. Saltman

ROWMAN & LITTLEFIELD PUBLISHERS, INC.
Lanham • Boulder • New York • Oxford

ROWMAN & LITTLEFIELD PUBLISHERS, INC.

Published in the United States of America
by Rowman & Littlefield Publishers, Inc.
4720 Boston Way, Lanham, Maryland 20706
http://www.rowmanlittlefield.com

12 Hid's Copse Road
Cumnor Hill, Oxford OX2 9JJ, England

Copyright © 2000 by Rowman & Littlefield Publishers, Inc.

British Library Cataloguing in Publication Information Available

Library of Congress Cataloging-in-Publication Data

Saltman, Kenneth J., 1969–
    Collateral damage : corporatizing public schools, a threat to democracy / Kenneth J.
Saltman
      p. cm.
    Includes index.
    ISBN 0-7425-0101-9 (alk. paper) — ISBN 0-7425-0102-7 (pbk : alk. paper)
      1. Privatization in education—United States.   2. Capitalism—United States.
I. Title.

LB2806.36 .S25   2000
379.1'5—dc21   00-032848

Printed in the United States of America

♾™ The paper used in this publication meets the minimum requirements of American
National Standard for Information Sciences—Permanence of Paper for Printed Library
Materials, ANSI/NISO Z39.48–1992.

Contents

Acknowledgments

I owe Henry Giroux a debt that I could never repay for his teaching and his wisdom—not to mention his kindness, patience, and generosity, of which his help on this book was but another example. I would also like to thank Ronald Bettig, Dan Marshall, and Pat Shannon for their generosity in reading and offering helpful comments and advice on the text. Great appreciation goes to editors Dean Birkenkamp and Christine Gatliff at Rowman for tremendous support. Enormous thanks to Robin Truth Goodman for her invaluable help and many hours spent in editing and discussing ideas. Special thanks to Heidi Leubs, who gave me an enormous stack of corporate curricula that she collected in her Chicago public school. Thanks to Alphonso Lingis for his inspiration, kindness, generosity, and hilarity. Thanks to Kathy Szybist, who offered many valuable ideas and insights, not to mention love and support. Thanks to my parents, Gilbert and Barbara Saltman. Thanks also to Stephen Haymes and all of my colleagues in the Social and Cultural Studies in Education Program at DePaul University. Thanks to Shawn Smith, Amy Smith, Heidi Henderschott, Sheila Macrine, Noah Gelfand, Kevin Bunka, Rick and Sally Ohanesian, Dalila Gonzalez, and Carlota Toledo.

Introduction

PRIVATIZATION AND THE ATTACK ON THE PUBLIC

In the United States and around the world, democracy is under siege. The current phase of capitalism is dominated by neoliberal imperatives for privatization, the liberalization of trade, and the contingent faith in the market as a universal solution to all social problems. Neoliberal privatization, the transfer of public institutions into private hands, is fundamentally at odds with democracy,[1] undermining the possibilities for democratic public life, political participation, and access to public goods and services.[2] Within the New World Order, public institutions from prisons to parks to welfare to constitutionally guaranteed public legal defense have been subject to a widespread fervor to privatize the public sphere.[3]

The omnipresent language and logic of the market works to redefine the public sphere as one more opportunity for profit. Within the current neoliberal order, business ideals of competition, accountability, and efficiency eclipse democratic concerns with the development of a critical citizenry and institutions that foster social justice and equality. Accusations that public schools are a "government monopoly" and terms such as *excellence, accountability, standards,* and *choice* shift public issues such as education to the terrain of business, where schools become businesses, students become consumers, and teachers become merely service labor.

Democracy involves the public struggle over values. The triumph of market language imposes a singular vision of the future and a singular set of values—namely, faith in capitalism. When this happens, there is nothing left to discuss. Authority becomes unquestionable, and dissent, the lifeblood of democracy, appears as disruption and threat. The only question is how to enforce this faith in the market. Education becomes a matter of enforcement. This emptying-out of democratic concerns and the singular emphasis on schooling for the corporate good appears as a renewed emphasis on testing and the standardization of curriculum but also as transformation of the public school on the model of the prison, the military, and the corporation. The growing logic of enforcement that is playing out through the public schools is part of a broader movement to militarize civil society, increase policing, create zones of "zero tolerance" but also to produce consent for this militarization in popular cultural forms like live-action cop shows, video games, action films, and mainstream coverage of political protests. In short, then, the highly antidemocratic rise of a culture of enforcement and violence results from the triumph of market values over human values.

Within educational reform debates and public discourse, the shift to market language makes an insidious appeal to common sense that naturalizes open calls for privatization. Particularly in the United States, corporate CEOs, the mainstream media, and the government announce that public education should serve corporate needs. Oil and junk food corporations declare that they are supporting public education as they infiltrate the curriculum with advertisements. Environmental curricula produced by Shell Oil focuses on the virtues of the internal combustion engine, "while offering pearls of wisdom like, 'you can't get to nature without gasoline or cars.'"[4] City after city installs business executives and career military personnel as school district "CEOs," while public school administration and culture at all levels are reformulated on the model of the corporation.

The corporatization of the curriculum and the school transforms the meaning of knowledge, citizenship, and work.

"A classroom business course . . . teaches students the value of work by showing them how McDonald's restaurants are run."[5]

Rather than teaching students to be citizens concerned with the well-being of others and the development of radically democratic communities, corporate curriculum trains students to be consumers.

Will is saving his allowance to buy a pair of Nike shoes that costs $68.25. If Will earns $3.25 per week, how many weeks will Will need to save? The Nike word problem and examples involving M&Ms, Oreos and fast-food restaurants appear in *Mathematics: Applications and Connections*, a sixth-grade math book published by Glencoe/McGraw-Hill. It is one of several text-books that mention brand names.[6]

Corporations are actively engaged in influencing knowledge content, sometimes in deadly ways.

Four years ago, the government of Indonesia, the financial giant Lippo bank and Mobil, Texaco, and Chevron hired the respected educational-publishing company Scholastic to create and distribute a high school social-studies curriculum called "Introducing Indonesia." The curriculum focused on Indonesia's natural beauty, traditional culture and the importance of US–Indonesia trade, and it described its political system as a "democracy" with "social justice for all the people." It never mentioned the dictatorial Suharto regime (then still in power), human rights abuses or other troublesome facts, such as the illegal invasion and annexation of East Timor (where a vote on independence was just held after a twenty-five-year struggle in which 200,000 people died). [The U.S. government gave $40 billion and arms and military training in support of Suharto, who murdered hundreds of thousands of Indonesian civilian political opponents in the '60s and '70s.][7]

Corporate curriculum trains students to be consumers and redefines schooling as another site of marketing to a captive audience. As in the previous example, the control over knowledge is about an economic elite justifying its plunder of nature, freedom, and basic human rights in the pursuit of profit.

"Exxon: Scientists and the Alaska Oil Spill," a lesson plan and video that praises the oil company's role in restoring the ecology of Prince William Sound while avoiding any discussion of what (or who) caused the Alaska oil spill in the first place.

"Energy Management and You: Learning to Use Energy Wisely" produced by Commonwealth Edison fails to distinguish its own responsibility for resource allocation and costs from that of individual citizens. "You can control the cost of energy by controlling how much you use." "By using energy wisely we can control how much of the fuels we use and how much we spend on energy bills." Commonwealth Edison also puts out a comic book called *Learning about Your Environment* which claims that "natural disturbances cause great changes in the environment" without mentioning how ComEd's nuclear and other power production causes great changes in the environment.[8]

Literacy, in the corporate curriculum, becomes about learning corporate logos.

An exercise book purports to teach third graders math by having them count Tootsie Rolls.[9]

A few months ago, a young couple in San Antonio, Texas, complained to their local school principal about their 5-year-old daughter's homework assignment to walk around and recognize corporate logos and then cut them out of the newspaper. It turned out that the school was using "Read-A-Logo," a new instructional reading software program that uses corporate logos in place of some common words.[10]

What is at stake here is also the meaning of history and the expansion of corporate culture into the government and throughout public services.

The United States Postal Service produces and distributes "Take a Field Trip through the 1980s" in "cooperation with" among others: Microsoft, Department of Defense Education Activity, International Society for Technology in Education, National Geographic Society, and the National Science Teachers Association.

> "The impact of technology and the desire to have fun are expressed in the entertainment, recreation, and lifestyle choices of the '80s. Students will explore the explosion of cable television and the growing popularity of the compact disc. They'll learn about video games, mountain bikes, and hip-hop culture—and much, much more. From the Horowitz concert to the San Francisco 49ers, from *The Bonfire of the Vanities* to Cabbage Patch Kids, your students will learn about the 1980s—and then create history themselves as they vote to commemorate their favorite subjects in stamps. It's the ideal way to excite kids about history and to Celebrate the Century!"

Focusing almost exclusively on consumer goods and services, the curriculum celebrates this era as the triumph of consumerism and defines education as entertainment and history as trivia. The curriculum lists the Postmaster General as Postmaster General and Chief Executive Officer.

Calls to privatize suggest that there is an inherent efficiency in the private sector. However, claims against the state couched in economic terms of efficiency should be understood as symptomatic of a broader growing disenchantment with the public sphere. Swelling antigovernment sentiment and popular distrust of all things public coincide with the shrinking of the public sphere. Political cynicism is at an all-time high and political participation at an all-time low. Participation in civic groups, from religious organizations to labor unions to women's and fraternal clubs, has declined across social class.[11] The reasons for the decline of the public include calculated efforts by conservatives to undermine public institutions as a way of upward transfer of wealth and power. These efforts include the mass-mediated production of a culture of cynicism in which individual agency can only be expressed through private participation in the market.

Though privatization does result in the reallocation of funds, predominantly in unfair ways, any assumption of scarcity driving privatization initiatives is unfounded. Decisions to increase military funding by billions of dollars while decreasing educational spending have less to do with scarcity than priority. The assertion that privatization derives from scarcity leads to misconceptions about where the blame is to be placed for unequal access, undemocratic practices, and growing disparities in wealth. Federal expenditures, despite rhetoric to the contrary, are distributed based on reasons other than need or the scarcity of funds. These reasons include political priorities, private corporate interests, and social values. These priorities, such as redistributing public resources to the private high-tech, military, and carceral industries, are largely supported by cultural pedagogies[12] expressed in corporate mass media.

In addition to concerted efforts by conservatives to privatize the public sphere, there are at least two historical crises through which the broader logic of capital is being expressed. The first could be called a "crisis of political identity" and the second could be called the "death of federalism."

The end of the Cold War has produced a national identity crisis and "national identity vacuum." With the dissolution of the Soviet Union, and with what political theorist Chantal Mouffe has called the resultant "crisis of political identity," the meaning of democracy has become increasingly struggled over. Neoliberal and neoconservative writers seized upon the fall of the Berlin Wall and the demise of the Soviet Union to claim that capitalism triumphed over communism. In the triumphalist rhetoric, democracy has largely become synonymous with liberal capitalism. Corporate mass media has seized upon the redefinition of democracy. For example, as a recent Winston cigarette advertisement put it, "Even Communists are Free to Smoke," revealing the extent to which freedom has been redefined as the freedom to consume mass-marketed commodities. In fact, this ad points to the extent to which freedom has not merely been redefined as the freedom to consume, but the freedom that comes with the commodity transcends politics and ideology. Consumerist freedom in this triumphalist discourse replaces political differences altogether. As *New York Times* foreign correspondent Thomas L. Friedman writes, singing the praises of American corporate domination in his "Golden Arches Theory of Conflict Prevention," "No two countries that both had McDonald's had fought a war against each other since each got its McDonald's. . . . And people in McDonald's countries don't like to fight wars anymore, they prefer to wait in line for burgers."[13] Friedman illustrates how the denial of the political that comes with capitalist triumphalism results in social issues rendered matters of enforcement and authoritarianism rather than democratic deliberation. As Friedman writes, "McDonald's cannot flourish without McDonnell Douglas, the designer of the U.S. Air Force F-15. And the hidden fist that keeps the world safe for Silicon Valley's technologies to flourish is called the U.S. Army, Air Force, Navy and Marine Corps."[14]

Capitalist formulations of traditional democratic political and ethical principles of equality, freedom, and citizenship stand to benefit the most privileged segment of the population, those already holding the most power. In this sense, the redefining of democracy in private and capitalist terms and the effacement of moral and political principles of equality have been the result not merely of the play of social forces but rather a concerted effort on the part of a ruling class that has succeeded in capturing the language of democracy and redefining it in private terms.[15] The rise of information technology and the intensified concentration of the control of communicational technologies and media production such as TV, newspaper, and Internet have assisted in the effort. The consistent material upward redistribution of wealth since the early '70s coincides with a consistent decrease in workers' real wages and also coincides with intensifying ideologies or pedagogies of consumption and individualism.[16]

The present historical moment is also seeing a political crisis that could be called "the death of federalism." As Frederic Jameson points out, the fall of the Berlin Wall and the so-called end of communism may in fact signal the death not of communism but of federalism.[17] The implications of such an interpretation are radical indeed and highly relevant here. If, in fact, as Jameson claims, the dissolution of the Soviet Union marks a death knell for federalism rather than communism, then we can understand the attack on the public sphere in the West as a global phenomenon long predicted by Marx's historical materialism as the inevitable outcome of the globalization of capital—the withering away of the state. The flexibility and power of transnational capital renders state borders porous or erased, as witnessed by the establishment of the European Union, the power of world trade organizations and agreements such as NAFTA (North American Free Trade Agreement), WTO (World Trade Organization), MAI (Multilateral Agreement on Investment), the IMF (International Monetary Fund), and World Bank, as well as by the growth of NATO (North Atlantic Treaty Organization).[18]

Jameson's thesis of the end of federalism seems to confront an intractable problem in the face of the U.S. federal government's thirst to return to Cold War levels of armaments. Bipartisan-supported military expenditure initiatives, justified on the grounds of the need for the United States to have the capacity to fight two regional conflicts, might seem to suggest that a militarily strong federal government signals the strengthening of federalism. Yet, increasing military investments, in fact, point to increasing privatization of public interests as Lockheed Martin, Boeing, and General Dynamics—corporate producers of military equipment—are profiting from the United States' and NATO's increasingly unilateral role as world cop for the New World Order. Growing federal spending on arms may bolster the antifederalism thesis when we understand antifederalism as the challenge to the nation-state posed by the globalization of capital which the U.S. military largely facilitates through direct coercion when the culture industry fails to produce adequate consent.

In short, then, antifederalism is taking the form of not only the transfer of power from federal governments to localities but the transfer of nonprivate international power (UN, World Court, Universal Declaration of Human Rights) to organizations and nations representing the forces of privatization—namely, global capital and a global capitalist class (United States and Europe, NAFTA, WTO, IMF, NATO). This antifederalist phenomenon must be understood as a result of the increasing transnationalization of capital.[19] Corporate sponsorship and influence of NATO's and multinational corporations' use of private militaries (such as Chevron's private use of Nigeria's military, which used helicopter gunships to massacre civilians protesting Chevron's policies) testify to the decline of the federal state and the open transfer of the military to the service of the multinational corporation. The privatization of the military does not have to take such an overt form. The government can wage war for corporate interests as it did, for example, in the case of the Gulf War. What Charles Derber calls the new "guilded age" of the '90s, with its endless mergers and rapid and unprecedented upward concentration of wealth, has resulted in the consolidation of the military corporate contractors into just three companies that lobbied for the expansion of NATO. In this sense, the turn to military spending is a form of social spending that is highly private and highly antipublic.

The privatization of the military is taking the form of (1) military expeditions such as the Gulf War to serve corporate interests such as oil; (2) the rise of private armies serving corporations (symptomatized not only by Chevron's actions but by private international security and "antiterrorism" services); (3) corporate sponsorship of military events such as the fiftieth NATO anniversary; (4) the consolidation of military corporate contractors; and (5) the United States' continued role as the world's number-one exporter of privately produced armaments.

The growth of privatization of the military needs to be understood in relation to an increasingly militarized view of civil society. This social militarization can be seen in recent Supreme Court rulings favoring increased police searches and limits on the rights of individuals to congregate publicly. This also appears in the rise of police documentary TV shows such as *Cops* and *America's Wildest Police Videos,* as well as mass-mediated celebrations of policing and high-tech weapons of war, which can be found as much in mainstream magazines and newspapers as in video games. These mass-mediated glorifications of raw power offer viewers the perspective of a missile headed for target, but they omit the grisly aftermath of shredded and charred human flesh. They show police officers busting working-class citizens, but they also omit the histories and social conditions, such as poverty and racist institutions as well as jobless and abandoned geographies, that produce the class of citizens these shows call criminals. Instead of showing histories, contexts, and aftermaths, these cultural products sell extracted spectacle to viewers so that the commercials can pitch commodities. These cultural forms function politically and pedagogically by promoting popular identifications with coercive power and by suggesting the structuring of social relations in authoritarian rather than democratic ways.

Militarization and corporatization have infected educational reform debates and the mass-mediated public discourse about education. Spurred on by mass-mediated representations, urban, largely nonwhite, working-class schools are increasingly subject to martial law in the form of surveillance cameras, police presence, metal detectors, chains, fences, and mandatory uniforms. Military personnel with no teaching experience are being installed as teachers and administrators. Superintendents who are retired generals are often being given the title of CEO. Chicago has opened R.O.T.C. high schools. The language of discipline and enforcement dominates reform debates over standards and curriculum, generally obscuring the relationship between structural, social, and historical conditions and the present state of public schooling. In fact, as this book goes to press the role of public education in assisting the relationship between the military and the corporate sector is beginning to surface in a more overt fashion. The U.S. Commission on National Security, also known as the Hart-Rudman Commission, has announced the inadequacy of the "two regional conflicts" thesis, which justified maintaining extremely high levels of military spending since the end of the Cold War. Despite the fact that the United States has no credible military threats, the new plan will increase and expand the military (and justify increased military spending) in multiple ways, focusing heavily on the role of publicly funded education and the military in protecting corporate wealth.

> Though established by Defense Secretary William Cohen, the panel placed heavy emphasis on economic and nonmilitary aspects of national security. The report recommends that traditional security agencies—State, Defense, CIA, and the National Security Council—work more closely with the treasury and commerce departments, as well as Justice and Transportation officials. State and local governments must be better integrated into preparations to defend against attacks on U.S. soil, the panel said. The report urges policymakers to make education a top national priority, particularly in math and science. It says the United States must create more advanced and effective forms of public–private partnerships

to spur technological innovations. The report devotes considerable time to discussing the emerging global economy and the United States' role within it. It says that although environmental and labor concerns must be addressed, they should not be allowed to block or reverse free-trade policies.[20]

Public education as a training ground for corporate workers is now being framed as an issue of national security suggesting that the well-being of the nation depends upon the well-being of the corporation. Such an understanding of public education openly envisions the state in the service of the private interest and profit.

We are witnessing what Stanley Aronowitz has called the gutting of the compassionate functions of the state. As federal responsibility for such public goods as social service provision and public schooling shifts to private corporations and state control, the federal government is increasingly rendered a disciplinary entity concerned primarily with military, policing, prisons, and courts. The new social logic can be seen clearly in the ways that youth become both casualties and commodities in the war on the public. As Betty Reid Mandell, among others, points out, millions of youth, who were the primary recipients of welfare, are the prime victims of its dismantling.[21] Their increasingly "at-risk" status transforms youth into commodities in a $21 billion for-profit social service market.

> While many non-profits are still reeling from cutbacks on social spending, for-profits are celebrating the fact that government outsourcing is still growing in so many areas.[22]

Who are these for-profits who have scored on the dismantling of social services for youth? One of the biggest poverty profiteers is big three military contractor Lockheed Martin, which is operating welfare-to-work schemes in four states. For-profit Youth Services International, purchased in 1998 by Correctional Services Corporation, makes over $100 million a year running juvenile detention "boot camps," subjecting youth to physically demanding military training. SunTrust Equitable Securities published a report on government spending in child welfare, juvenile corrections, and special education entitled "At-Risk Youth . . . A Growth Industry."[23] What is particularly egregious about these examples is that after youth have been put "at risk" by the denial of public services, such as the late AFDC, they then become an investment for the same people who lobbied for the destruction of the same public services that were designed, when properly supported, to keep youth out of risk. In the words of Henry Giroux, the politics of investment in youth is being replaced by a politics of containment.

The new draconian image of a federal government purged of its compassionate dimensions well serves fiscal conservatives and libertarians who argue that government is inherently oppressive and that the public good is only accelerated through decreased market controls and the transfer of public money to private business. What is particularly startling about the present moment is that neoliberals share with neoconservatives a faith that the corporate good *is* the public good. Neoliberals have taken the lead not only at dismantling and privatizing the welfare state but at "streamlining" government to take a corporate appearance and rationale, pushing antilabor fast-track agreements, and showing unmitigated support for corporate power at the expense of public concerns with the environment, public health, and education. At stake here in current battles over schooling and privatization is the threat that the broader privatization movement poses to a democracy concerned with broad-based public welfare.

The implication of the convergence of these factors—the logic of capital with its privatizing, individualizing tendencies, the crisis of political identity, growing antifederalism, a right wing readily seizing on the historical moment, and the cultural construction of capitalist pedagogies—is a snowball effect of antipublic sentiment. The media-constructed crisis of education exemplifies this snowball effect.

The idea of a crisis of public education has a long history but gained significant attention in 1983 with the publication of *A Nation at Risk,* a report created by policy analysts tied to a conservative administration bent on dismantling public education. However, the crisis rhetoric in the policy report did not work to undermine public support for public education until it was picked up by the mass media. An onslaught of negative reporting about public education followed, with an unfairly represented public education being wrongly blamed for every social ill from the failure of big business to compete globally, to the loss of jobs, to a rise of youth murder.[24] Critics of the crisis, such as David Berliner, have shown the crisis to be a farce masking consistent improvement and progress in public education. Others—such as Alex Molnar[25]—have confirmed Berliner's claim of improvement yet pointed to the way the constructed crisis of education has undermined public funding of this vital public good.

The undermining of confidence in public education can hurt it in very real terms by depriving public schools of the resources needed for high quality schooling. Furthermore, mudslinging against the schools serves the mass media in the short run because bad news sells. Bad news in education plays on and produces fears about youth endangerment and national weakness. It also serves the papers ideologically, in that attacks on public institutions further the class interests of those who benefit from privatization. In other words, claims for the failure of public institutions function to justify privatization initiatives. Because American mass media is monopolized by a few tremendously powerful and wealthy interests, news assaults on the public sphere serve the economic interests of the owners of the mass media by undermining public confidence in public entities and by shaping public opinion.[26] The undermining of the public sphere has played a large role in opening the doors for privatization initiatives in education despite the proven failure of privatization experiments in the '70s and despite their antidemocratic tendencies.

Critical educators and cultural workers should not despair in the face of current assaults on the public sphere and, more specifically, attacks on public schooling. Despite the seemingly deterministic movement of history emerging from the insights of historical materialism, despite the current "crisis of the political" facing Western democracies, despite a right wing intent on seizing the opportunities presented by the current historical juncture and undermining public goods—teachers and other cultural workers must recognize that they are not merely the inheritors of history but that they, too, make history. Social structures such as capitalism, white supremacy, and patriarchy operate through culture and language. As such, culture and language are key sites of struggle over the ways that social relations are structured. Social relations do not have to be organized by oppressive structures. They can be transformed in more egalitarian, less oppressive ways. Teacher practices always speak to future social visions, even utopian ones.

This book offers teachers tools for the tasks ahead: (1) to comprehend the rapid privatization of public education; (2) to contest the privatization movement in order to defend public education as a democratic public space; and (3) most important, to situate antiprivatization efforts within the reconstruction of public education as a part of a broader reconstruction of critical citizenship and democratic public life.[27] This task demands the recognition that teacher practices are inextricably linked to broader social and political contexts. This book offers teachers and cultural workers a public language and framework in which to critique privatization. It encourages teachers to work for the expansion of a public sphere rich in social services, dedicated to human values before market values, and responsible to the public good over the private pursuit of profit.

In what follows, I consider the privatization arguments from the perspective of a democracy concerned not only with economic prosperity and individual freedom but also with both economic equality and cultural recognition. In this context democracy refers not merely to the right to vote or to a limited sense of political participation. Rather, democratization entails the extension of equal social relations throughout all spheres of society. Before discussing educational privatization specifically, however, I would like to delineate briefly the distinctions between different uses of privatization in order to (1) insist that although contemporary visions of privatization can take very different meanings and have different underlying justifications, they do share certain assumptions, and (2) to lay the groundwork for criticizing dominant versions of privatization from a democratic framework—the work of the first chapter.

Paul Starr distinguishes three visions of privatization: economic, cultural, and neoconservative.

By far the most influential is the vision grounded in laissez-faire individualism and free-market economics that promises greater efficiency, a smaller government, and more individual choice if only we expand the domain of property rights and market forces. A second vision, rooted in a more socially minded conservative tradition, promises a return of power to communities through a greater reliance on social provision on families, churches, and other largely nonprofit institutions. Privatization, in this view, means a devolution of power from the state to ostensibly nonpolitical and noncommercial forms of human association. Yet a third perspective sees privatization as a political strategy for diverting demands away from the state and thereby reducing government "overload." This last view, identified particularly with recent neo-conservative thought, does not necessarily conflict with the other two—indeed, some advocates of privatization draw on all three—but each vision suggests a different framework for analysis and policy.[28]

The economic vision of privatization differs markedly from the cultural and neoconservative visions, in that of the three it does not view privatization as a means to a greater social good but rather views privatization as an optimal social arrangement itself. Efficiency, a small government, and more individual choice do not themselves form a political referent. They are elements of a social situation defined principally by a "free market" economic arrangement. In the cultural and neoconservative visions of privatization, as Starr outlines them, privatization remains a tool for some greater social good. In the economic vision, privatization is both that greater social good and the means to it. Heightened individualism, greater personal freedom, and more unfettered economic opportunity are the "social goods" that privatization seeks to further. However, aside from the questionable ability of privatization to achieve these goals, the economic vision of privatization, unlike the other two, lacks any sense of collective purpose or communal good. The economic vision of privatization does not refer to some broader political or ethical sense of the social good, such as a democratic way of life or greater social and economic equality. Within this view democracy is only useful if it furthers a free market economy. As well, the metaphor of economic health functions to replace the notion of a common good. Since Starr wrote this over a decade ago, this economic vision of privatization has far eclipsed the other two in prevalence and has skillfully used the other two when necessary.

One of the gravest dangers of the economic vision of privatization involves the way power is wielded in a liberal democracy such as ours. In a state driven principally by economic concerns, those with the greatest wealth assume the greatest power. While a democratic state should serve the interests of all citizens, a state such as ours with radically unequal distributions of wealth provides that those with the most wealth dictate the conditions of the rest.[29] Recent neoliberal plans to place a portion of social security in the stock market well illustrate both the shift of the public/private distinction and the market logic shift that defines the public in terms of the private. When social goods become discursively linked to the success of private industry, the good of the corporation appears to be the social good itself.

In light of increasing disparities in wealth and income, such a collapse of the public and private is really a form of upward economic distribution. Furthermore, citizenship and political responsibility become defined by individual contribution to the interests of the Fortune 500 companies. Workers' rights and race, class, and gender equality are subordinated to concern with the bottom line as the public good disappears or is defined in private ways. The obvious antidemocratic tendencies of this change are apparent in the ways that the economic and cultural interests of most citizens are served neither by such an arrangement nor by the upward redistribution of power that accompanies such a redefinition of the public. When the ideal of economic health eclipses democratic ideals of equality, it becomes possible to place economic concepts on a higher plane. Terms such as efficiency, competition, and price, as well as a notion of quality informed principally by economic considerations, replace ethical and political considerations. Concomitantly, market language and logic come to dominate the terms of public debate. This is precisely what has happened in the field of education. One disastrous consequence of this is the increasing difficulty of framing educational issues in terms of a democratic tradition and discourse.

EDUCATIONAL PRIVATIZATION

As Jeffrey Henig points out, the privatization movement and the educational reform movement are closely related, even though public officials have been among the leading spokespersons for educational reform, the language, symbols, and specific policy proposals of the dominant strain in the contemporary education-reform movement have been imbued with the same suspicion of government and collective enterprises that the privatization movement manifests. Like proponents of privatization, education reformers look to economic theory and corporate practice for their models.[30]

While the meaning of privatization depends upon the context and the institution in question, in the context of American public education, privatization can be understood as a transfer of responsibility for the delivery of educational services from a local, state, or federal government to a private corporation. While the responsibility for providing a good or service shifts to a private interest in educational privatization, usually governments retain ultimate responsibility for the outcome.

Educational privatization takes many forms. The most extreme form of educational privatization calls for the complete dismantling of public education and the wholesale replacement of public schools with private schools. Extreme privatizers claim that market forces can provide better-quality schools than public education, that market forces can provide universal education, and that the market will yield greater educational equity than the public schools can. Reagan's and, more recently, Gingrich's calls for dismantling the U.S. Department of Education and "deregulating" education for corporate takeover are symptomatic of this view. This position, which views the market as a panacea, goes beyond economist Milton Friedman's initial proposal for privatization in the 1950s.

Friedman's position, which more typifies contemporary calls for privatization, advocated a more limited form of privatization yet radically questioned one principal assumption about public education. Namely, he challenged the idea that the government should be a direct provider of education. In Friedman's vision the government still levies school taxes and pays for education; however, the government no longer owns and runs the schools. The schools themselves would be privately owned and run. In addition to the government financing privatization, the government would impose some set of rules on schools to ensure a certain level of quality. Schools would be licensed by the state the way that individuals are licensed to fish or drive.

Framing education within the terms of microeconomics, Friedman characterized schools as lazy monopolies. He compared public education to profit-driven industries and suggested that injecting an element of competition into public education would drive up quality by making schools compete for students. Parents would shop for schools much the way they shop for bread or toilet paper, comparing price against quality. Friedman's market-based proposal, microeconomic language, and call for vouchers have formed the basis for the school choice movement. I discuss these aspects in greater detail in chapter 2 when I deal specifically with school choice. With regard to educational privatization more generally, Friedman's ideas and imagery impacted the educational reform debates dramatically by shifting the terms or terrain of the debates into the realm of economic language and logic. By characterizing public education as a monopoly rather than as a social good, he opened the door to countless conservative policy analysts and theorists to justify the dismantling of public education and the transfer of the task of schooling to private interests on the economic grounds of efficiency, competition, consumer choice, and price.

In the context of this work, educational privatization refers to two initiatives: (1) tax credits or educational vouchers given by the government to families to be spent on private or public schools, and (2) "contracting out public schools or school systems to be run by for-profit companies."[31] Hence, vouchers, charter schools, and performance contracting all fall within the purview of educational privatization.

A less overt but possibly more insidious form of educational privatization concerns what Henry Giroux has called "the ideology of corporate culture."[32] This differs from the attempt to relocate the ownership and control of the public schools to the private sector. The ideology of corporate culture can be understood as a coordinated set of antipublic values that function pedagogically to form the conditions for intensified privatization initiatives.

> As the rise of corporate culture reasserts the primacy of privatization and individualism, there is an increasing call for people to surrender their capacities for engaged politics for a market-based notion of identity, one that suggests relinquishing our roles as social subjects for the limited role of consuming subjects. Similarly, as corporate culture extends ever deeper into the basic institutions of civil and political society, there is a simultaneously diminishing of noncommodified public spheres—those institutions engaged in dialogue, education, and learning that address the relationship of the self to public life, social responsibility to the broader demands of citizenship, and the development of public spheres that invest public culture with vibrancy.[33]

In chapter 3 I discuss in greater detail the rise of corporate culture in education in the context of the commercialization of the public schools. At this juncture I want to stress that privatization and the culture of commercialization, as well as the commercialization of culture, should not be viewed separately. Rather, they feed each other: corporate pedagogies build consuming subjects and antipublic institutions. These institutions, in turn, breed corporate pedagogies and a corporate-defined sense of identity. However, this circuit of privatizing pedagogies should not be viewed with hopeless abandon. The circuit of privatizing pedagogies can be broken by individuals, such as teachers, producing democratic pedagogies and democratic identifications. Individuals can challenge privatization policies, defend public institutions, and create new public entities. My last section offers teachers ways of challenging the language of the market to express democratic ideals and to expand the public sphere.

In chapter 1 I detail a number of justifications for educational privatization. These claims and metaphors are used by profiteers as well as right-wing policy analysts and academics to justify both kinds of privatization initiatives—the attempt to transfer the public schools to private interests and the attempt to steep students and teachers in a corporate culture. The first section of chapter 1 takes seriously the privatization metaphors, and the second section explains what is wrong with applying market language to public schooling in a democracy. Chapter 2 focuses specifically on the language, logic, and history of school choice. This discussion of the market metaphor of choice examines competing versions of school choice to understand what kinds of social visions are embedded in them and, further, to mine them for elements compatible with a possible democratic theory of choice concerned with ideals of pluralism, equality, and human rights.

Chapter 3 examines how the struggle over public resources is playing out in public schools with the rise of commercialization. Using the case of the "Coke Day" suspension of a student in suburban Georgia, this chapter considers the implications for democracy of both the role of private enterprise in public spaces and the rise of consumer identities formed through corporate cultural pedagogies. As well, this chapter considers the possibilities for resistance and democratic struggle on the part of students, teachers, and other cultural workers. Chapter 4 looks at the growing militarization of urban, largely nonwhite public schools to understand the connections between private social vision and the formation of a carceral state for marginalized segments of the population. I reveal the ways that privatization is expressed through enforcement-minded, anticritical, and overly methodological teaching. As well, I examine the intensifying social climate of "law and order" and how that is playing out in public schools to the detriment of many citizens and the material benefit of a select few.

In chapter 5 I show how a constructed crisis of the "out-of-control" teacher works in conjunction with the discourse of youth innocence to reassign blame for public school failures to individual teachers as well as students and to eliminate social responsibility. Such reassignment of blame, which gets redefined through a political and symbolic scapegoating of women in a discourse of deviancy, justifies current unequal resource allocations to the benefit of privileged populations and also wrongly suggests that school reform can be strictly a matter of methodology. This discussion runs through the media spectacle surrounding the case of Mary Kay Letourneau and the film *The Faculty*, as well as an inaccurate scare article published in *Educational Forum*. All of the chapters are tightly bound by their insistence on the need to recapture a democratic language for public schooling. They are also united by their insistence on the need to rethink public education as part of a broader struggle for education as a vital public sphere committed to radically egalitarian and yet diverse social transformations.

NOTES

1. For a clear and detailed explication of neoliberalism, see Noam Chomsky, *Profits Over People: Neoliberalism and the Global Order* (New York: Seven Stories, 1999).

2. In the context of this work, I distinguish public from private in terms of control over property, wealth, and the means of production, as well as control over deliberative power and cultural production. Public goods and services are controlled and largely owned not by private, for-profit individuals and groups but by those served by these same goods and services. Private goods and services are owned and controlled to provide profit for the private owners. I want to distinguish my use of *private* as a way of expressing antipublic control from the concept of privacy, which refers to psychological states and the autonomy of individual subjects.

3. My use of the term *public sphere* draws on the following: Jürgen Habermas, *The Structural Transformation of the Public Sphere*, trans. Thomas Burger (Cambridge: MIT Press, 1989); Nancy Fraser, "Rethinking the Public Sphere: A Contribution to the Critique of Actually Existing Democracy," in *Habermas and the Public Sphere*, ed. Craig Calhoun (Cambridge: MIT Press, 1992); Nancy Fraser, *Unruly Practices* (Minneapolis: University of Minnesota Press, 1989); Nancy Fraser, *Justice Interruptus* (New York: Routledge, 1997); Chantal Mouffe, *The Return of the Political* (London: Verso, 1993). Habermas's public sphere, with its universalized notion of juridical ethics, is useful for recognizing the need for communitarian ideals. Habermas's ideal is, however, limited by its liberal embrace of consensus and defense of Enlightenment rationality. As Giroux writes, "There is an undertheorization of how democracy gets translated differently in diverse cultural landscapes or how the constraints on agency, not to mention communicative action and deliberative possibilities, are structured differently among marginalized groups." Giroux, "Counter Public Spheres and the Role of Educators as Public Intellectuals: Paulo Freire's Cultural Politics" (unpublished draft, 1999).

4. Steven Manning, "The Corporate Curriculum," *The Nation* (27 September 1999): 17.

5. Manning, "The Corporate Curriculum," 17.

6. "Math + "Ads" = Trouble," *Time for Kids,* 17 September 1999.

7. Manning, "The Corporate Curriculum," 17.

8. Manning, "The Corporate Curriculum," 17.

9. Manning, "The Corporate Curriculum," 17.

10. Manning, "The Corporate Curriculum," 17.

11. Carol Ascher, Norm Fruchter, and Robert Berne, *Hard Lessons: Public Schools and Privatization* (New York: Twentieth Century Fund, 1996), 4.

12. My use of the term *cultural pedagogies* draws on Henry Giroux's notion of the teaching that cultural forms accomplish through cultural production and distribution. This involves not only what culture teaches but how representations produce identification with particular subject positions and social interests. Cultural pedagogies, then, can refer here to how cultural forms function politically to consolidate or contest power and to construct identities. Pedagogy within this view is not restricted to schooling but needs to be understood in an expanded sense to what happens in culture. As Giroux writes, "The pedagogical dimension of cultural work refers to the process of creating symbolic representations and the practices within which they are engaged. This includes a particular concern with the analysis of textual, aural, and visual representations and how such representations are organized and regulated within particular institutional arrangements. It also addresses how various people engage such representations in the practice of analysis and comprehension. The political dimension of cultural work informs this process through a project whose intent is to mobilize knowledge and desires that may lead to minimizing the degree of oppression in people's lives." Henry A. Giroux, *Border Crossings: Cultural Workers and the Politics of Education* (New York: Routledge, 1992), 5.

13. Thomas L. Friedman, *The Lexus and the Olive Tree: Understanding Globalization* (New York: Farrar, Straus, Giroux, 1999), 195–196.

14. Friedman, *The Lexus and the Olive Tree,* 373.

15. The redefining of democracy as capitalism took a more overt form following the collapse of the Soviet Union. The triumphalist political rhetoric of George Bush's New World Order speeches in the early '90s asserted the triumph of a democracy defined by free markets over communism. Concomitantly, academic and popular press publications proclaimed the end of history characterized by the final victory of liberal capitalist democracy. Francis Fukuyama's *The End of History and the Last Man* was at the forefront of these triumphalist claims. Critical responses to the end of history thesis included Jacques Derrida's *Spectres of Marx,* Charles Derber's *What's Left,* and writings by Noam Chomsky and Stanley Aronowitz, among countless other intellectuals. In the context of education, see Giroux's "Corporate Culture and the Attack on Higher Education and Public Schooling," Phi Delta Kappa Education Foundation, Fastback 442 (1999), for a discussion of the political use of the triumph of liberal democracy claims. For excellent discussions of the struggle over the meaning of democracy in mass media, see Robert W. McChesney, *Corporate Media and the Threat*

to Democracy (New York: Seven Stories, 1997) and Don Hazen and Julie Winokur, eds. *We the Media* (New York: New Press, 1997).

16. See "A Dialogue with Noam Chomsky," *Harvard Educational Review* 56, no. 4 (Summer 1995): 127–144. Reprinted in Pepi Leistyna and Steven Sherblom, eds., *Breaking Free: The Transformative Power of Critical Pedagogy* (Cambridge: Harvard Educational Review, 1996): 109–128.

17. Frederic Jameson, "Notes on Globalisation as a Philosophical Issue," in *The Cultures of Globalization*, ed. Frederic Jameson and Masao Miyoshi (Durham: Duke University Press, 1998).

18. For an excellent discussion of the relationship between global economics and education, see Peter McLaren, *Revolutionary Multiculturalism: Pedagogies of Dissent for the New Millennium* (Boulder: Westview, 1997).

19. Here I use the terms *federalism* and *antifederalism* loosely in order to explain the global character of the privatization movement—namely, the transfer of power from the public to the private.

20. "Panel Labels Two-War Strategy Outdated," *USA Today,* 19 April 2000, A9.

21. Only 4 million of 13 million recipients of AFDC were adults. See Mandell's "Poor Women and Children Need Welfare," in Charles P. Cozic, ed., *Welfare Reform* (San Diego: Greenhaven, 1997), 20.

22. William Ryan, "The New Landscape for Nonprofits," *Harvard Business Review* (January/February 1999): 127–136.

23. Ryan, "The New Landscape for Nonprofits," 129.

24. The scapegoating of education for social ills parallels the scapegoating of working white middle-class mothers. Both are represented in mass media as causing a breakdown of the family. In fact, these narratives of the school and the mother as dangerously "out of control" come together, as I discuss in the final chapter.

25. Alex Molnar, *Giving Kids the Business* (Boulder: Westview, 1996), 9. See also Laurence Ogle and Patricia Dabbs, "Good News, Bad News: Does Media Coverage of the Schools Promote Scattershot Remedies?" *Education Week* (13 March 1996): 46. See Svi Shapiro's "Public School Reform: The Mismeasure of Education," *Tikkun* 13, no. 1: 51–55.

26. For a discussion of this, see Murray Edelman, *Constructing the Political Spectacle* (Chicago: University of Chicago Press, 1988). Also see Thomas Frank, ed., *Commodify Your Dissent* (New York: W. W. Norton, 1997) and Hazen and Winokur, eds., *We the Media,* and McChesney's *Corporate Media and the Threat to Democracy.*

27. This goal emerges from the insights of the long progressive history and the insights of the critical tradition, which understand the aim of democratic schooling as concerned with giving students the tools to critically engage with realities in order to remake them. On the relationship between democratic schooling and critical citizenship, see Henry A. Giroux, *Schooling and the Struggle for Public Life* (Minneapolis: University of Minnesota Press, 1988).

28. Paul Starr, "The Meaning of Privatization," *Yale Law & Policy Review* 6, no. 6 (1988): 20.

29. See *The Left Business Observer* (July 1997): 3. As of 1995 "the richest 0.5% of the population claimed . . . 28% of net worth almost as much as the bottom 90% of the population (32%) . . . If you strip out the principal residence, the major repository of middle-class wealth (but one not easily redeployable in the capital markets: most people won't sell the house to buy stocks), the top 0.5% pulls well ahead of the bottom 90%. The richest 10% of the population—about 10 million households—owned 84% of the stock and 90% of the bonds held by individuals (including that held indirectly through mutual funds). The democratization of ownership supposedly brought about by mutual funds has a long way to go." In part, because of the massive power wielded by the media industry to shape public opinion, construct identity, and form desires—to produce public pedagogies—the concentration of wealth in the hands of an economic elite translates to economic and cultural agendas favorable to few at the expense of most.

30. Jeffrey Henig, *Rethinking School Choice* (Princeton, N.J.: Princeton University Press, 1994), 6.

31. Ascher, Fruchter, and Berne, *Hard Lessons: Public Schools and Privatization,* 6–7.

32. Giroux, "Corporate Culture and the Attack on Higher Education and Public Schooling."

33. Giroux, "Corporate Culture and the Attack on Higher Education and Public Schooling."

1

Educational Privatization and the Assault on Public Schools

THE DANGERS OF EDUCATIONAL PRIVATIZATION

There are two principal dangers of educational privatization. The first concerns the fact that on its own terms, namely market terms, privatization does not seem to reduce educational costs or increase quality. In fact, as a number of scholars have demonstrated, in most cases the opposite is true. Presently, very little evidence exists to support any claims that privatization improves education or reduces its cost.[1] Mounting evidence suggests that, among other things, privatization increases bureaucracy, increases costs, increases the potential for abuse and corruption, decreases public oversight, and decreases the stability and reliability of high quality services.[2] At first glance this question of efficacy may seem to be the real issue. In fact, the question of efficacy resides squarely within the purview of the market metaphor and eclipses more fundamental questions about the purpose and goals of schooling in a democratic society. In other words, the second principal danger of educational privatization concerns the way that its focus on efficacy obscures broader social concerns with ethical and political justifications for public schooling.

David Labaree has written that modern educational debates have swung between two basic purposes of schooling. One views schooling for social efficiency while the other, in the tradition of the reconstructionists, sees schooling for democratic equality. Schooling for social efficiency understands schools as places where competent workers are made. Schooling for democratic equality sees the school as a place for the creation of democratic citizens capable of consensual deliberation with the potential for social transformation. In other words, schooling for social efficiency aims to make students who can fit into the social order, while schooling for democratic equality seeks to make students capable of transforming it and democratizing it further.

1

Labaree finds the American origins of schooling for democratic equality in the common school movement of the nineteenth century. He explains that the movement sought to unite the polity in the face of changing social circumstances—the market and increased diversity.

The leaders of the common school movement saw universal public education as a mechanism for protecting the democratic polity from the growing class divisions and possessive individualism of an emerging market society. The common schools, they felt, could help establish a republican community on the basis of a shared educational experience cutting across class and ethnic differences. These schools could also help prepare people to function independently as citizens in a democratic society. This vision is at heart an inclusive one, grounded in political rather than economic concerns.[3]

Labaree explicates what he believes to be a radical shift in the educational debates. No longer is schooling justified only on the grounds of democratic equality or social efficiency but now largely on the grounds of a third goal—social mobility. Labaree is worth quoting at length on what he views to be an unprecedented contemporary shift in education.

From the perspective of this goal [social mobility], education is not a public good but a private good. If the first goal [democratic equality] for education takes the viewpoint of the citizen and the second [social efficiency] takes that of the taxpayer, the third takes the viewpoint of the individual educational consumer. The purpose of education from this angle is not what it can do for democracy or the economy but what it can do for me . . . [I]n an educational system where the consumer is king, who will look after the public's interest in education? As supporters of the two public goals have long pointed out, we all have a stake in the outcomes of public education, since this is the institution that shapes our fellow citizens and fellow workers. In this sense, the true consumers of education are all of the members of the community—and not just the parents of schoolchildren. But these parents are the only ones whose interests matter for the school choice movement, and their consumer preferences will dictate the shape of the system.[4]

Labaree is absolutely right about the dangers of the market logic that has come to dominate the educational debates. He is also correct about the problems with the way education is justified on grounds of social mobility.

I think, however, that the educational goal of schooling for social mobility needs to be understood as a strategy, one strategy, that has been successfully yet very specifically deployed by those advocates of a broader strategy—namely, the antidemocratic upward redistribution of material, cultural, and symbolic wealth. In the privatization debates, advocates of privatization, school choice, and vouchers hold out the promise of social mobility to working-class and nonwhite students. Social mobility claims by the right and by neoliberals are largely a way of making up for the market's complete indifference to the well-being of citizens and the right wing's lack of concern with equity. The promise of social mobility is tied to a highly individualized, meritocratic free market ideal, suggesting that the market provides for those worthy and hardworking.

Social mobility, however, is not the current dominant justification for privatization. Privatization is still generally justified on the grounds of social efficiency as well as social mobility. Privatization initiatives, when they are pitched to privileged populations, do not appeal to social mobility goals for privileged students for whom well-funded public schools provide upward social mobility or a reproduction of privileged social status. When addressing privileged populations, arguments for privatization usually appeal to social efficiency. In reality, privatization initiatives do not stand to remove public education as a public good from wealthy white suburban kids. For the parents of these kids, the failures of public schooling are elsewhere and *those people* might just benefit from a dose of the discipline of the market. As I discuss in chapter 4, the defunding and underfunding of urban and nonwhite schools is tied to the discourse of discipline. The sorry state of many urban nonwhite schools is often portrayed in racist ways as an example of lazy, undisciplined nonwhites.[5] This reassigns responsibility for impoverished neighborhoods and schools from the broader society and powerful privileged populations to the victims of these unequal social conditions and unequal educational and employment opportunities. For a great number of urban, poor, and nonwhite students, social mobility is a farcical notion antithetical to their lived experience of public school as a penitentiary-like containment center. Social mobility, then, is a market metaphor, one of *many* market metaphors that shift education from being thought of as a social good to being a private entitlement or even a private consumable. The metaphor of social mobility as well as the other market metaphors are tools in a conservative effort to redefine the terms of the educational reform debates.

DISMANTLING THE MARKET METAPHORS

Proponents of educational privatization typically justify their arguments on one or a combination of seven basic market metaphors: (1) efficiency; (2) competition; (3) the failure of public education; (4) equity; (5) accountability;

(6) democracy;[6] and (7) individual freedom of choice.[7] This chapter presents these justifications and criticizes them.

All of the previously mentioned arguments for privatization rely upon the metaphor of the market for their force and even for their intelligibility. Prior to the shift to the language and logic of the market in policy and academic circles, the reform debates were characterized by a concern with equity and universal education. "Until the 1980s concerns about equal educational opportunity for all students still dominated the national dialogue."[8] In fact, early privatization initiatives were framed in this language. The emergence and consequent triumph of the market metaphor and the shift in the educational reform debates mark the success of a broader redefinition of democracy and democratic citizenship as fundamentally economic rather than social, individual rather than communal, and a matter of technique rather than collective vision.

Efficiency

The argument for efficiency states that education has been suffering from the sluggish and inefficient bureaucracy of the state. Writes Janet Beales of the Reason Foundation, which promotes free enterprise, "Since the cost of labor is often lower in the private sector, overall efficiency is enhanced by using the private sector, particularly for labor-intensive organizations, such as education."[9] In this view, the problems of education, such as less than optimal test scores in science and mathematics, can be solved by injecting education with a healthy dose of market-induced efficiency. The argument for efficiency relies on a direct comparison of schools with business. Privatizing schools through the use of tax credits or vouchers will make schools compete for students. According to the argument, this will lower costs while driving up quality. Schools unable to compete will naturally fail and this will weed out the bad schools, leaving only good schools. The argument for efficiency is tied to the idealization of competition as a means to greater efficiency. For example, Philadelphia schools are tested for progress in standardized tests. Schools are forced to compete for inadequate resources that are withdrawn if they fail to meet certain scores. This process, known as "reconstitution," shuffles entire schools of teachers from poor schools to other poor schools as punishment for poor performance in the competition for funds.

Similarly, advocates of performance contracting argue that school systems or schools should contract out to private corporations because private entities, with a view to maximizing profit, are always more efficient than public ones. This efficiency can be relied upon to decrease red tape and hence decrease overhead. In keeping with the market metaphor, advocates of privatization claim that increased efficiency will also improve quality by forcing different contractors to compete with each other for the best results measured by standardized tests.

The efficiency metaphor was launched by the Reagan administration. Upon his election, Reagan first proposed a series of radical changes, including the dismantling of the U.S. Department of Education, the implementation of vouchers to use public money to pay for private and parochial schools, and the goal of bringing prayer into public schools. Reagan's plans were sharply contested by Democrats and even Republicans who were still largely faithful to the idea that public schools should serve the common good. Many fought Reagan's plans to breach the separation of church and state. Unions clearly perceived the voucher proposal as an attack on labor, while liberals and conservatives were wary of what seemed to be an overt privatization scheme. In the early '80s private profit from the use of public money had yet to be redefined as a public good. Instead, it was seen as a form of corruption. Trickledown theory and supply-side economics had yet to fully conquer common sense. In the early '80s, Reagan, facing fierce opposition, retreated on all fronts only to return with a more clever privatization strategy in the late '80s.

By January of 1988, Reagan was no longer trying to abolish the Department of Education. Instead he began championing "school choice." Rather than advocating the private use of public money, such as vouchers to pay for private and parochial schools, he shifted tactics and championed the use of public money for public school choice. While I discuss this in more detail in chapter 2, I raise this history here because Reagan's next move had a tremendous impact on the education reform debates by redefining them in terms of efficiency. In short, Reagan successfully unlinked magnet schools from the issues of race and equity and connected them instead to market ideals of efficiency, "excellence," and competition.

He accomplished this by first claiming magnet schools as proof of the success of a market-based approach to education and the model for a school choice movement. In reality, magnet schools were nothing of the sort. Magnet schools had traditionally been developed out of the civil rights struggles to counter racial segregation. Like busing, magnet schools were the product not of a free market but rather of authoritative government action. Furthermore, magnet schools were the result of a government principally concerned not with consumer choice but rather with racial equity and countering a 400-year legacy of vicious racist discrimination and inequality.

By associating the concept of choice with ongoing activities in the public sector, the Reagan administration launched a multidimensional counterattack. It preempted the kinds of legal and philosophical challenges that had stymied previous efforts to enact choice plans that included parochial schools. Simultaneously, it defused the potent racial issue, addressed concerns about administrative feasibility, furthered its effort to shift debate from issues of equity to issues of effectiveness, linked its educational-reform stance to its central ideological commitments to New Federalism and privatization, and—perhaps most important— set the stage for the claim that empirical evidence supported its proposals. This repackaged vision of educational choice had so immediate and broad an appeal that it became a central element in George Bush's presidential campaign and subsequent domestic program.[10]

While vouchers were first formulated in contemporary times by Milton Friedman, they were first enacted in America in Southern states as a racist strategy to resist federal desegregation efforts. Many factors enabled the administration's successful unlinking of equity and race from vouchers. These included an administration that believed that the unchecked pursuit of racial equality had distorted the federal domestic policy agenda. Changing demographics left half of the national constituency five years old or younger when *Brown* v. *Board of Education* forged an unbreakable association between vouchers and bigotry. In addition, white America was growing weary of racial equality issues, due to representations that framed the expansion of a black middle class and increased exposure of blacks in popular culture as evidence that racism was no longer systematic and institutional. Furthermore, the misperception that affirmative action had effectively compensated for historical inequalities and the unlinking of vouchers from their racist history were facilitated by a nationwide recovery of white supremacist sentiment linked to a reawakened nationalism.[11]

The Reagan and Bush administrations and increasingly the mass media used rhetoric and media images to associate criminality, deviance, and social pathology to nonwhite Americans while simultaneously associating wholesomeness, family, and industriousness with whites. The films of the '80s testify to this effort.[12] Ideologically, efficiency as a concept has been used since the '80s to justify a redistribution of wealth and cultural valuation. In light of relative declining national prosperity, an emigrating industrial economy, a steadily declining real wage, and record income for fiscal elites, the imperative for individual efficiency has functioned to scapegoat nonwhite, poor, working-class, and middle-class individuals for the declining level of wealth. Nonwhites, in particular, bear the brunt of this scapegoating effort by being characterized in media culture as parasitic, lazy, violent, and a threat to an efficient social order. The language of efficiency has no place for considerations such as basic human rights to food, clothing, shelter, medicine, and education.

Furthermore, the language of efficiency is thoroughly ahistorical, denying the conditions that produce unequal social relations.

As human beings become increasingly viewed in economic terms—students as commodities or clients, teachers as practitioners, administrators as business executives—it becomes easier to place economic value and rank on human life and human services. The dismantling of welfare and the creation of workfare serve as good examples of this logic. Human beings must justify their very existence in economic terms or risk being expelled from the community. In New York City in 1999, Mayor Rudolph Giuliani ordered the police to arrest homeless people for sleeping on the street. The mayor gave homeless people a choice to turn themselves in for forced labor or be arrested. The fact that the federal AFDC budget prior to being cut was about 1 percent of military spending suggests that the dismantling of welfare had little to do with saving money.[13] It had, in part, to do with a redefinition of human value in economic terms.[14]

The educational privatization movement of the mid- to late '90s needs to be understood in the context of a broader class war that could be marked by the election of a Republican Congress in 1994. The dismantling of welfare, the creation of workfare, and the calls for prison labor and for the privatization of social security, public space, and education point to a broader attack on the welfare state and hence a fervent effort to restrict noneconomic human activities. As Christian Parenti points out, the '80s and '90s saw the right strike back against the achievements of labor and the civil rights movement in the 1960s. An expanded social wage and increased regulation on business achieved in the '60s was attacked largely, as Parenti points out, through attempts to "re-discipline labor: that is, on assaulting the living standards and general power of working people."

> In the US this has meant that older forms of absorbing and co-opting the poor and working classes with welfare and employer concessions had to go. These forms of social democratic and Keynesian intervention—while keeping class struggle contained, providing stimulus, and legitimizing the market system— had the unfortunate side-effect of empowering the laboring classes in ways that were destructive for business profits. . . . With strong unions, inexpensive higher education, and ample welfare, the classes that sell their labor had less reason to take poorly paid, dangerous, or dirty work. To truly discipline labor, *all* alternative avenues of sustenance had to be closed. Thus we had the Reagan-Bush-Clinton welfare enclosures, the assaults on the environmental regulation, the rights of labor, consumers, and the poor; in short, the near total evisceration of New Deal and Great Society forms of downward redistribution.[15]

Considering that many of the antipublic reforms such as welfare reform, prison labor, and public school privatization do not save money and often cost the government more money, these schemes need to be understood as a part of the ideological component of class warfare. "As the class structure polarizes in the interests of restored profitability, the state must step in to deploy and justify police terror, increase surveillance, and overuse incarceration."[16] Like these more overt forms of coercion, the privatization of education in its various manifestations is part of a broader upward redistribution movement on the part of an economic elite. Privatization not only allows elites to profit from a once off-limits sector, but it also results in the exclusion and containment of segments of the population. Such an insight allows a way to think about how the expansion of prison-like school reforms serves as a form of direct coercion (a politics of containment) within a racialized and gendered class war, and it allows a way to think about how the corporatization of curriculum and the expansion of corporate culture produces consent for rule by business interests. Understanding that the carceral industry, the defense industry, and the privatization of education are part of a class war allows progressive educators and cultural workers to think in terms of linking diverse material and cultural struggles. For example, struggles to transform education in democratic ways need to be linked to struggles against the growing police state and against the prison business, as well as to struggles for labor and the environment, and all of these struggles need to be linked to the broader social struggle for radically democratic transformation.

Generally, the imperative for efficiency in all domains drains experience of its depth, richness, and texture; reduces nature to its use-value and hence plunderability; and transforms others into objects, thereby robbing them of their intrinsic human value. Specifically with regard to education, the efficiency metaphor has functioned to perpetuate the myth that the quality of education has nothing to do with fiscal expenditures. Nothing could be further from the truth.

The efficiency argument for educational privatization does not address the question of what schooling is for in a democracy. It assumes that schools transmit knowledge much the way banks dispense cash. As such, the only relevant criterion for schools is an optimal balance between standardized achievement and cost. Privatization for greater efficiency presumes a universal sense of socially valued knowledge. However, privatization advocates do not all agree on what knowledge matters most or even on what methods are most effective at transmitting it. For example, the knowledge and methods of acquisition championed by E. D. Hirsch differ radically from those of black nationalists who favor privatization in reaction to a public school system that has seemed ineffectual for their needs. The metaphor of efficiency covers over differences such as these by suggesting that privatization will offer optimum outcomes for all participants. As Jeffrey Henig has pointed out, this has proven to be an effective strategy for mobilizing privatization sentiment. The broad base of appeal for privatization relies upon vague notions that in time will be found to represent opposing values. Unfortunately, these fundamentally different values will emerge only after privatization has begun. A democratic form of deliberation rather than a knee-jerk reaction would enable an open discussion of social values. Market metaphors generally, with positive-sounding terms such as choice and efficiency, appeal to people because they promise an easy and universal solution to problems that in fact require messy and slow democratic resolutions.

The language of efficiency ignores the struggle over cultural values that characterizes a pluralistic state. A genuine democracy must provide for power sharing by different groups. For groups to share power means that they are able to put forth their own group values and interests. Of course, there must be limits to those group values that do not promote a broader social well-being. For example, in a liberal democratic state there are limits on groups and individuals that transgress the boundaries of individual freedom and human rights. However, in a liberal democratic state such as ours some groups have a disproportionate amount of power to control social values. Hence, the pursuit of excess wealth holds far higher social sway than other social values, such as universal access to basic needs like food, clothing, shelter, education, health care, and medicine. This arrangement benefits wealthy and ruling-class individuals at the expense of the bulk of the population. In a meaningfully democratic state, the pursuit of certain groups' interests would be checked when they deprive other groups of the basic need to participate in a deliberative democracy concerned with all citizens' well-being. In a genuine democracy education becomes a basic need for citizens to have the tools to participate meaningfully in furthering the common good.

The metaphor of students as consumers works with the metaphor of efficiency to redefine education as an industry like any other. This opens the door to education as a market for investors to make money. As Alex Molnar has brilliantly shown, the transformation of the school into one of the hottest new investment sites has had a tremendously detrimental impact on the quality of curriculum, has drained time from useful classroom learning, and has promoted an air of hucksterism and commercialism. Youth are seen not as democratic citizens in the making but rather as potential customers. In the words of Henry Giroux, students are redefined as consuming subjects.

The efficiency argument parallels the way economic news has come to be framed on television and radio. Events such as a drought, a rise in employment, or a war are typically discussed in relation to how they will effect consumers or create jobs. For example, the city of Philadelphia recently offered the Disney Corporation a million dollars to open a Disney retail complex downtown. The justification for the gift was that it would create local jobs. Of course, these few retail Mcjobs will offer minimum wage, no benefits, and no unions. Conceiving of education as a market allows all social values to be subsumed to the ideal of economic efficiency.

One basic fallacy of the efficiency metaphor is that the private sector is more efficient than the public. In fact, in many cases just the opposite is true. Every American is familiar with the scandalous disasters the U.S. military has endured in contracting out to private corporations for goods and services. Usually, events such as the Pentagon's purchase of a $400 toilet seat get attributed to government inefficiency. In fact, one of the high social costs of privatization is the loss of government oversight over the production process. By virtue of being public, public institutions are highly scrutinized by the public. Private corporations are less scrutinized than government. Their private status allows the hiding of records and profits. If public funds are paying for a service such as education, the public should be able to see where people's money goes. In educational contracting numerous scandals have surfaced, revealing how private corporations' evasion of public oversight has resulted in resource allocation that would never pass public scrutiny. For example, in Texas, a struggle over the public right to information from Channel One resulted in the revelation that the corporation had been evading its tax obligation to the very district that had allowed Channel One to profit from it. It was also discovered that the equipment that Channel One had put in schools as a part of its contract was worth a fraction of what Channel One had claimed. The company was found to be making massive profits on funds that should have been used for public school education.[17]

This raises a fundamental problem with the idea of performance contracting of a public good. Why should an individual or group of investors profit from what should be reinvested back into the schools themselves? In the cases of Baltimore's contract with EAI and Boston University's Chelsea School District experiment, both corporations refused to divulge their financial records to the public. It turned out that they did so for a reason. EAI was incapable of showing performance comparable with the public schools, despite spending much more money per student. This increased expenditure was garnered from two places: It was drained from other schools in the school system, and it came from cutting qualified teachers and replacing them with uncertified and less-experienced aides. Chelsea School District's "partnership" with Boston University resulted in the underfunding of the school district with no improvement in quality. Where did the money go? To Boston University president John Silber's offices.

Another inefficiency of privatization comes from corporate culture. Top executives are accustomed to flying around their regions in jets, being picked up in limousines, and making high salaries and bonuses as well. The money for such jet-setting must come from somewhere. Unfortunately, it comes from the children these companies are supposed to be helping. Because of the way public schooling is funded, poor, working-class, and nonwhite districts that are already underfunded are most targeted for "help" from profit-seekers. The transformation of public schools to private ones needs to be understood as a form of social redistribution of wealth and power: Funding is transferred from the public to the wealthiest citizens "investing" in education; as well, deliberative power is exported from the local district to the corporation, the owners of which seldom use the schools they run.

Another major inefficiency of privatization comes from the need for more administration. Ironically, the call for privatization is often justified on the grounds that public bureaucracies are constrained by red tape. The experience with performance contracting revealed that privatization actually increases red tape.

> Performance contracting was introduced to circumvent educational bureaucracies and eliminate the red tape so evident in many schools. Accountability would be clear-cut: success or failure at coaxing student gains in achievement. Yet performance contracting seemed to make life more complicated in many ways. Teachers complained that contracting increased their routine clerical work, as they responded to requests for regular reports on students' progress. The need for coordination between school administrators and officials in the companies also caused problems, and it required an increase in the number of individuals in administrative roles.[18]

As Alex Molnar points out, educational privatization almost always involves not only the upward redistribution of wealth but the redistribution of control over schooling. When corporations take control of a school, they seldom are located in the geographic area of the school. Local control over decisions is exported to corporate headquarters land. This has the detrimental effect of local people being subject to the whims of outsiders who have no personal investment in the results of their decisions. For example, if the CEO of a company like EAI decides that in order for EAI to make more money in Hartford or even to be competitive with other area schools he must reduce the number of qualified teachers and replace them with low-paid aides, he can do so with no ill effects on his own family, who may live on the other side of the country. From the perspective of microeconomics, what may appear to be an efficiency can be a disastrous inefficiency from the perspective of a democracy that values local control over decisions affecting the community.[19]

The argument for efficiency relies on a direct comparison of schools with business. Schools are not businesses. One of the great fallacies of the market metaphor is the assumption that schools are businesses or are very similar to businesses. Businesses exist for the individual profit of owners and shareholders. They seek fiscal profit and are fundamentally directed by the bottom line. Businesses are privately held entities and benefit private parties. Schools are not fundamentally concerned with providing a fiscal profit (despite the intentions of many profiteers). Schools exist to provide education, which is primarily a public good.

The microeconomic logic of privatization supposes that individuals act only in their own interest. In this view government exists for the purely negative function of limiting individuals from pursuing their own benefit at the expense of others. However, individuals do not act only in their own self-interest. In fact, individuals act in the interests of others at their own expense all the time. Not only do people make sacrifices for others, but also they recognize that often to act in the interest of others may be limiting in one way only to benefit oneself in other greater ways.

The microeconomic logic of the market cannot understand the teacher who stays after school to help her student grasp long division. This teacher gives of herself not out of selfish interest but because she feels richer as a person by giving her time and her knowledge—giving unconditionally, with no expectation of return. One would be hard-pressed to find a teacher who teaches for the money. Most teach because they love to give of themselves. Teachers feel deeply satisfied when they ignite their students' passion for learning. The ebullient form of passionate teaching cannot be understood by the logic of the market. Market logic wrongly presumes that people harbor a hardened cynicism toward others, that every relationship is defined by the thought "What's in it for me?" People do not generally think this way. Public entities differ from businesses in that they are provided by the public to serve the public. Individual contributions to public entities are meant to benefit the public.

In education, a dangerously antidemocratic trend has intensified that views public entities as a source of profit for private interests. This is tied to a broader societal shift that views the health of private corporations as identical with the health of the nation. One need only turn on the television news to confirm the prevalence of this view. One very clear illustration of the falsehood of this presumption is the recent trumpeting of the economic boom of the late 1990s. Television and newspaper reporting suggests that the economy has been very successful in creating record economic growth. This growth measures corporate profit, which reflects an elite minority of the population. The real wages of the majority of the population have steadily declined, benefits have decreased, the workweek has grown, and massive corporate firings used to fuel the boom have forced millions of individuals into self-employment and lower-quality work. Low unemployment figures do not account for the decreased quality of work. Rather, they reference only the number of people employed. Were economic success measured by those in society worst off, we would quickly realize that America in the late '90s has been experiencing a depression.

Specific to education, schools have been redefined as ripe for corporate "partnerships." Steadily decreasing corporate taxes since the end of the Second World War have depleted tax bases and left public schools with a funding crisis. As well, "corporate welfare" has grown to record proportions. Public monies have been increasingly used to finance corporations at public expense. Politicians typically justify this on the grounds that the health of the industries being supported benefits the public. Corporations, having depleted the tax base, want to "help" schools by providing "curriculum" (advertising for these corporations thinly veiled as curriculum), paying schools for advertising space, or actually buying schools and trying to turn a profit with them. These profiteering schemes threaten to shrink the public sphere by transforming public goods into private investments. But perhaps more insidiously, as Jeffrey Henig has pointed out,

> the real danger in the market-based choice proposals [and in privatization more generally] is not that they might allow some students to attend privately run schools at public expense, but that they will erode the public forums in which decisions with societal consequences can democratically be resolved.[20]

I have already mentioned the danger of the loss of local control that usually accompanies educational privatization. More broadly, educational privatization results in a deterioration of democratic space. The spread of privatization leaves fewer spaces for democratic decision making, deliberation, and consideration of bolstering the common good. The result of this erosion of public forums is a transfer of power to private interests. Those who already have the most power and privilege are allowed to set the terms of debate for everyone else. Those groups already marginalized by being underrepresented, and silenced through historical inequalities, will have diminished power and place without the benefit of a public sphere. The erosion of the public sphere results in at least two major calamities. First, decision making, policy, and a vision for the future become monopolized by those with the most power. The disappearance of the public results in a might-makes-right form of governance. In a liberal democracy this translates to the maintenance of a plutocratic elite.

Second, the centralizing of power will inevitably result in a higher degree of disenfranchisement, social exclusion, and violent instability. Resentment toward those in power will inevitably be expressed in more violent forms, such as domestic terrorism and even simple crime. The erosion of popular forums for the expression of power, coupled with the denial of basic needs for the majority of the population, breeds cynicism and hopelessness, resulting in social malaise and a culture of despair that in turn breeds self-destructiveness and violence.

Competition

The 1983 publication of *A Nation at Risk* marked a significant shift in the educational reform debates. The agonistic metaphors of war and business guided this publication commissioned by Reagan's secretary of education. The report begins, "If an unfriendly foreign power had attempted to impose on America the mediocre educational performance that exists today, we might well have viewed it as an act of war."[21] The report framed education in terms of global competition—a metaphor typical of national competition for strategic and economic power. Calling on the business community to form "partnerships" with education, the report suggested that there was a crisis of education requiring radical reform. Because the crisis was framed in economic and militaristic terms, the solution would be sought in those domains.

A Nation at Risk put educators on notice that they had better cooperate with business in building a "world class" system of education. Japan's economic successes in global business in the '80s scared Americans much the way Sputnik had in the '50s. In both cases education was blamed for America's lost ground to its adversary.

The metaphor of global competition has served politicians and policymakers by providing them with a "pocketbook issue" with which to mobilize constituent support. Educational privatizers link the metaphor of global competition to economic performance in order to enhance a sense of a crisis of public education. According to Thomas Toch, this link is

the principal reason that the nation supported the push for excellence in education so strongly; more than anything else, it was the competitiveness theme that defined the education crisis in the nation's eyes.[22]

Of course, as anyone familiar with the education reform debates knows, the push for *excellence* that Toch identifies has not been simply about excellence. The term has been part of a rhetorical strategy by conservatives to bolster an educational agenda hostile to equity and friendly to a conservative curriculum. *Excellence* is a positive-sounding catchword with universal appeal. Who can argue with excellence? However, excellence in education does not refer to excellent services for students, excellent working conditions for teachers, or an excellent ideal of teaching for democratic social change. *Excellence* refers to an instrumentalized notion of teaching deriving from the history of scientific management, a heavy reliance upon standards, and a curriculum oblivious to the knowledge of different groups. An empty word, *excellence* can defend a culturally conservative curriculum such as Hirsch's Core Knowledge or it can justify a fiscally conservative curriculum principally concerned with training students for the business world. The term has no unified meaning in a positive sense. Rather, its meaning derives negatively from what it is hostile to—namely, universal quality education, a curriculum concerned with equity, social justice, and progressive values. The market metaphors of competition and excellence contribute to a crisis attitude toward education and justify claims for the failure of public education. These claims are without an empirical basis. This points more generally to the fact that metaphors such as the market metaphors often stand in for real evidence. They often bridge the gap between prescriptive claims and empirical evidence.

The metaphor of competition found in the *A Nation at Risk* report, in Molnar's view, functioned to scapegoat education for structural economic failings that had nothing directly to do with education. It provided a justification for corporate entree into the educational arena by positioning business as a model of success. Concomitantly, business leaders were given a loud voice in educational policymaking.

> The enthusiasm with which executives and their political allies responded to *A Nation at Risk* was not surprising. Its underlying logic cast America's enduring economic crisis as primarily a symptom of the failures of public education. Its self-assured, bombastic tone helped direct public attention away from any careful assessment of the extent to which the economic problems facing the United States were a function of structural problems in the economy, the consequence of deliberate corporate strategy, or a result of government policy turned toward business. It also helped create a political climate in which the pronouncements of business leaders assumed preeminent status in the debate over educational change.[23]

The market-based framing of reform and the loud voice given to business leaders reflect a fundamental shift in the logic characterizing the relationship between corporations and schools. "Good schools contribute to everyone's economic well-being" became "How can public schools make individual corporations profit?"[24] This shift in thinking opened the gates to the commercialized reforms of the '90s. As Molnar writes, "If the profit motive was a stowaway carefully hidden when the corporate reform ship set sail during the 1980s, it is now at the helm."[25]

The metaphor of global competitiveness resonates with the imagery of sport, as well as with an older nationalist sentiment. In the '80s this older nationalist sentiment, which in part fueled the competition metaphor, was also tied to racism. The Japanese were posited in the press as a threat. Apocalyptic newspaper articles were published every time a Japanese investor bought a building in New York. In fact, Japanese acquisitions of American real estate trailed behind British and German. Evil Japanese businessmen served as the enemy on the silver screen in films such as *Black Rain* and *Die Hard.* Yet at the same time, Japan's rigid, hierarchical, authoritarian educational system was admired by countless writers and trumpeted as the secret to their economic success. In the '80s the Japanese were represented in the mass media as successful in business due to their self-sacrificing culture. Countless education articles appeared attributing Japanese economic success to a strict and disciplined classroom with a rigid hierarchical structure and to vicious high school competition for limited university spots.

The metaphor of competitiveness was characterized by a jarring contradiction in the '80s. It was linked to both a heightened hyperindividualism and rugged nondependence and, paradoxically, a demand for individual sacrifice to the nation and self-discipline. The war- and sports-based metaphor of competition, in part, functions to overcome these seemingly contradictory pedagogies.

The use of the metaphor should be understood as part of a scapegoating effort on the part of business and mass media. America's failing ability to compete in the global market of the '80s was blamed on education when it was the failure of business itself that was to blame. Not only does America have one of the best-trained workforces in the world, but also American companies spend less on worker training than foreign rivals and "what money they do invest in education goes disproportionately to the upper ranks of employees."[26] Corporate reformers such as the outspoken Louis Gerstner of IBM keep the focus on schools and off the failure of business to promote the well-being of most citizens. Furthermore, the health of the domestic economy cannot be explained with reference to a single factor. The economy is a dynamic and complex phenomenon. To blame new workers for the failure of the economy makes little sense anyway. New workers do not make the decisions that determine the direction of the economy. As Alex Molnar points out, the constructed "skills crisis" was, paradoxically, followed almost immediately by the creation of "workfare." First, education was blamed for a weak economy by producing unskilled workers and for compromising the competitiveness of American business. Then, welfare was dismantled and the unemployed were told that there was no reason that they should not be working. This schizoid stance on "worker quality" belies the reality that representational tactics re-assign blame for the failures of a business economy to those public institutions and individuals subject to its whims, vicissitudes, and incapacities. By the mid-'90s the rhetoric of the skills crisis had disappeared. So had the rhetoric about the yellow menace and the glorious discipline of Japanese schools, as the Japanese settled into a lingering economic malaise throughout the '90s.

The Failure of Public Education

The claim that public education has failed has remained one of the most powerful arguments given by privatizers. Simply put, public education has failed the nation by making it less competitive than it could be and has failed students by not providing equal access to high-quality education. The argument draws on aforementioned competition claims as well as claims for equity suggesting that the monopoly on public schooling has had its chance and that now it is time for the market to be given an opportunity to succeed. Evidence of the failure of public education is garnered from reports of abominable standardized test scores on basic skills. Conservative advocates of vouchers and performance contracting point to progressive books such as Jonathan Kozol's *Savage Inequalities* to illustrate their argument that public schooling has resulted in the worst kinds of racial inequalities in the realm of education and to suggest that only the most radical reform, free market reform, can promise any hope of change.

The terminology and the logic of the failure of education often accompany descriptions of public education in market language as an unnatural monopoly. Joseph P. Viteritti, for example, writes

> Last March, Kurt Schmoke, the innovative mayor of Baltimore, spoke out about the need to provide alternatives to parents and "liberate American students from the public school monopoly." Education, he regretfully noted, "used to be a poor child's ticket out of the slums; now it is part of the system that traps people in the underclass."[27]

In Viteritti's view, public education is culpable for reproducing unequal social conditions. The American dream ideal of upward mobility provides the basis for his argument. On a "level economic playing field" individuals would have equality of opportunity to work for an improved economic status. According to the author, public education has failed to provide individuals with the basic skills necessary for upward mobility. In this view, American society and the market economy are understood as fundamentally just. Education is responsible for allowing individuals the opportunity to take advantage of a fundamentally fair situation.

Privatization advocates often use the competition and efficiency metaphors to justify an argument that public education has failed and thus should be subject to radical market reform. This argument relies upon the logic and language of traditional economics, which holds that protecting unprofitable business results in noncompetitive industry. Noncompetition leads to inefficiency and poor quality. Often, claims that public education has failed are coupled with the Milton Friedman description of public schools as an unfair monopoly. The cry of "monopoly" inverts the causality of poor performance by some schools. As Jonathan Kozol explains in *Savage Inequalities,* the issue of public school performance cannot be seen apart from its relationship to systematic underfunding. As Kozol extensively illustrates, public schools prosper in places that are well funded from having a high tax base. Likewise, the poorest schools are in the poorest areas and suffer from other forms of material and economic deprivation as well. In short, the failure of some public schools to provide high-quality education does not derive from the failure of public schooling as an institution. The problems derive from the method of funding. As David Berliner has shown, the quality of public schooling in general has been rising steadily throughout the century, in terms of both student performance and access to education.

This is not to say that American public education is not suffering from a serious funding crisis. However, the solution to improving poor public schools entails a change in the way schools are funded, not in trashing public schooling or in turning it over to the very same system responsible for its crisis. The funding crisis of education owes its existence in large part to the corporate community that has failed the public schools by providing a steadily shrinking tax base to fund public schooling. This corporate tax drain hurts schools by reducing government resources. Molnar writes,

the tax and social policy priorities championed by corporations made it more difficult for public schools to succeed and reduced governmental resources to help achieve a more wholesome and safer environment for poor and working-class children outside the school. Senator Howard Metzenbaum saw the problem and argued for measures that would discourage business from exacting from communities preferential tax treatments that undermine the local tax base: "In speech after speech, it is our corporate CEOs who state that an educated, literate work force is the key to American competitiveness. They pontificate on the importance of education. They point out their magnanimous corporate contributions to education in one breath, and then they pull the tax base out from under local schools in the next. Businesses criticize the job our schools are doing and then proceed to nail down every tax break they can get, further eroding the school's ability to do the job."[28]

The extent of corporate tax base depletion in the second half of the century is startling. While schools are typically funded from local taxes, the decline in corporate contributions to the federal tax burden reveals that while America's poorest schools have been struggling for basic materials, America's wealthiest individuals have been profiting. In the 1940s corporations paid 33 percent of the federal tax burden. By the '60s this was down to 27 percent; 15 percent by the '80s; and, currently, corporations contribute less than 10 percent of the federal tax burden. Of course, individual tax share had to rise drastically to make up for the profits of America's wealthiest individuals. While in the '40s individuals contributed 43 percent to the national tax burden, by the '80s this had risen to 73 percent, and by the early '90s, 76 percent.[29]

The crisis of education is largely a constructed crisis that emerged with the *A Nation at Risk* report. The report marked a definition of the crisis as economic.

After the publication of *A Nation at Risk,* the alleged catastrophic failure of public schools became an article of faith in boardrooms, policymaking circles, and the media. The economic importance of public education became the most potent argument for education reform in the 1980s and 1990s. If schools didn't do better, executives shouted, the economy would continue to crumble. Again and again, business leaders told the public that international competitors were beating American businesses because foreign schools did a better job of educating their young.[30]

Many studies have shown that precisely the opposite is true. The declared crisis of education is based in four claims, typically: standardized test scores, international comparisons, evidence of popular dissatisfaction, and anecdotal reports from businesses about the difficulty of finding well-prepared employees.[31] In response to the first claim, Berliner has shown that an insignificant drop in S.A.T. scores obscures a success of public education. According to Berliner, educators should be

filled with pride that we have played a major role in the achievement of two of America's most prized goals of the 1960s—a higher high school graduation rate, particularly for minority children, and increased access to higher education. We accomplished both goals with a loss of only a few correct answers on the SAT.[32]

International comparisons have suggested that American public education is among the most effective mass education systems.

> According to recent research, the monochromatic picture of American public school failure when compared to schools in other countries may also be misleading. American nine-year-olds read better than anyone in the world except Finnish nine-year-olds, and American fourteen-year-olds come almost as close, according to studies by the International Association for the Evaluation of Educational Achievement.[33]

Truly spectacular successes of American public education never make the papers. For example, a Rand study revealed that Title I funding for compensatory education for disadvantaged students since the 1960s has resulted in dramatic improvements by black and Latino students that far exceeded expectations.[34] Laurence Ogle and Patricia Dabbs have detailed the lopsided treatment of education news in the mainstream media. They found that, generally, reports of public educational progress do not get covered while decreases in test scores and other bad news consistently receive coverage. They draw an important conclusion from this. The media's bad-news-only reporting tactics might influence the public to give up on public schools or hinder the public from being able to identify real problems.[35]

Not only has American public education shown steady improvement, but also authoritative government action directed at specific aims has shown the most improvement.

> The declaration of an educational crisis, however, rests on a partial and one-sided reading of the available data. Just as powerful are figures that tell a somewhat different story: one of progress in expanding educational achievement, lowering dropout rates, improving performance as measured by some tests of reasoning and substantive knowledge, narrowing educational differences between whites and racial minorities, and maintaining a stable base of public support and appreciation. These victories are not complete; most fall short of what we might hope for. But several demonstrate steady progress, and a few are dramatic. Moreover, some of the clearest gains are in precisely those areas that had been collectively identified as high priorities warranting authoritative government action.[36]

Key issues with regard to the failure of education claim are: How does the claim function? Whom does the claim benefit? What does such a claim justify? Who is making this claim?

The claim for the failure of public education, like the other market metaphors, needs to be understood as a part of a concerted effort by the political right to justify the upward redistribution of wealth and cultural value. Crisis rhetoric is a scare tactic that ultimately comes to justify the most damaging forms of antipublic, antilabor reforms. The language of crisis stirs emotions and results in knee-jerk policy reactions. Meaningful deliberation takes time. Reactive policy measures are short-sighted and usually fail to comprehend the systemic nature of social ills. According to Henig, three reasons to reject the crisis claims are: (1) the crisis obscures different values; (2) it undermines the capacity for collective agency; and (3) it short-circuits public deliberation and has the potential to influence structural changes that may not be so easy to reverse.[37] I am in agreement with Henig that the market-based reform plans can be highly antidemocratic and that this fact is obscured by the drive for immediate reaction.

Equity

Related to the claim of the failure of education to assimilate students into a fundamentally just social order is the claim that public schooling perpetuates inequalities while privatization offers the possibility for overcoming them. For privatization advocates, racism is a matter of unequal economic opportunity. Privatization, they argue, would create greater opportunity by resulting in higher-quality schools and presumably would put schools wherever parents have a need. Those public schools, in urban, working-class, working-poor, and nonwhite places, that do not provide high-quality education should lose funding and be allowed to fail to make room for private schools.

This argument is highly ironic in light of the history of educational theory critical of reproductive models of capitalist schooling. Since the progressive era, educational theorists have pointed out that capitalist schooling reproduces social inequalities. Schooling should, they contend, transform social relations in a more egalitarian fashion. The work of progressives such as George Counts was renewed in the '70s by Bowles and Gintis and refined and developed by Apple, Giroux, Young, Whitty, and others. Only recently have conservatives begun to bastardize the socially conscious theories of progressives to argue for reactionary agendas. Hirsch's *The Schools We Need and Why We Don't Have Them* characterizes such willful attempts at using a model of social criticism to justify the maintenance of a cultural and economic elite.

Arguments for privatization based in equity are wrong for the following reasons: (1) Private schools are not better than public schools; (2) the current social order is not fundamentally characterized by racial equity, so assimilation into it does not promote equity; (3) even if the current social order were not thoroughly racist, the ideal of social mobility does not provide for the bulk of the population, it promotes a lottery mindset; (4) privatization is tied to a history of racism that it cannot so easily shake; (5) racism is not merely an economic issue that can be overcome by expanding economic opportunity; and (6) even if racism were merely an economic issue, privatization would not help because it intensifies class inequalities.

Privatization advocates such as Joseph Viteritti justify their claims on the grounds that private schools are better than public schools. Significant evidence suggests that precisely the opposite is true. Ascher, Fruchter, and Berne in *Hard Lessons* detail the disastrous experiments with performance contracting in the '70s. These experiments revealed that when teaching services were contracted out to private firms, student performance declined. More recent disasters in Hartford and Baltimore have confirmed these findings. In addition to worse test results, the experiment with performance contracting revealed other detrimental effects of privatization: large class sizes, increase in red tape, and curricular uniformity at odds with difference.[38]

> . . . company-run classrooms tended toward greater uniformity than comparable classrooms in the school system at large. This was in part because the curriculum stressed materials-based instruction and in part because the pressure on the companies to raise achievement caused a certain inflexibility in their approaches to education: the capacity of contract teachers to adapt to the variety of specific needs of different classrooms actually decreased, even though the companies claimed to offer "individualized instruction."[39]

Standardized curricula meant to lower overhead are at odds with an educational philosophy that takes seriously democratic ideals of pluralism and the valuation of difference.

As Pedro Noguera presciently predicted in 1994, competition will most likely create bad private schools. This is in large part due to the facts that private schools will be underfunded and not held to the same standards as the public schools, as well as to the fact that private schools will rely on non-unionized, undertrained teachers who are overworked and assisted by unskilled aides. A 1996 article by Chester Finn confirms privatization critics' worst fears. Touting charter schools as a success, Finn details what sounds like an unmitigated failure: low teacher pay; heavier teacher workloads; "cramped budgets"; inadequate administration; inadequate physical sites; hazy or non-existent curricula; noneducators running the schools; a lack of food services, transportation, and extracurricular activities; and a need for thousands of hours of unpaid "parental" work (read female labor) to support the school.

Finn points out that the tenuous grip charters have on funding means that many will fail midyear. He blames the government for this. Unbelievably, Finn attempts to paint a rosy picture of this bleak and destructive trend that gives public funds to private "partnerships." For example, he claims that teachers are happier working more for less money and without union representation or job security. This is because they "are willing to make trade-offs, including minimal facilities and modest pay, in return for personal and professional fulfillment." This fulfillment includes being what Finn calls a jack-of-all-trades: mopping floors and repairing the school. Charters often cannot afford basic janitorial services.

These inferior charter schools just so happen to be serving a disproportionate number of poor and minority students. "In the six states with the most charter schools, minority youngsters, who make up 31 percent of pupils in regular public schools, comprise 40 percent of charter school enrollment (17 percent black, 15 percent Hispanic, 5 percent Native American, 3 percent Asian)."[40] Why might this be the case? Wealthy communities would not stand for such shoddy public schools. Because charters arise in areas where the public schools are already severely underfunded and suffering from countless problems, charters can be presented as a legitimate alternative that in some cases may offer some benefits. In reality, poor and minority populations that have already been deprived of basic public goods and services due to unfair distribution of public resources are being targeted as the recipients of a scheme meant to look like progress yet with no real advantages over the underfunded public schools they are meant to replace.

Finn sounds surprised at the large number of groups interested in "partnerships" with charter schools. It should come as no surprise, given the commercial opportunities that fast food chains, real estate developers, and other businesses see in developing partnerships with the public schools. These associations open the possibility for social agenda setting, implementing business-friendly curricula, and educating children to become consumers at formative stages in life. For example, "the Minnesota New Country School, in the farming town of Henderson, resembles a Kinko's, with children at personalized work stations and teachers moving from child to child,"[41] training kids for corporate culture and initiating them into the laws of consumption. At the same time businesses are able to promote an image of social responsibility by disingenuously promoting these "partnerships" as acts of philanthropy or community betterment. A genuine act of social responsibility on the part of corporations would be to voluntarily raise corporate tax rates and earmark increased revenue for public schools.

Traditionally, U.S. society has been dependent upon public schooling for a variety of answers to societal problems. According to Pedro Noguera, this public reliance upon public schools is increasing.

[C]ommunities across the country increasingly are looking toward their public schools for solutions to a growing list of social problems. Whether the issue is drugs or the environment, violence or sexually transmitted diseases—more often than not, the search for solutions involves turning to the public schools to find ways to influence popular attitudes on matters of critical social importance. Hence, rather than becoming expendable, in many respects U.S. society is becoming increasingly dependent upon public schools as one of the few remaining viable social institutions that can be relied upon to address a variety of social issues.[42]

One grave danger of public schools falling to privatization is the erosion of public forums for democratically deliberating on and resolving difficult issues.

Another great danger of privatization involves the likelihood that it will re-segregate the public schools. Some laissez-faire fiscal conservatives argue that the market itself will desegregate by allowing parents, regardless of race, to shop for the best schools. This argument has little merit, considering the history of desegregation: massive federal resources were required to achieve integration. Tremendous resistance to integration, particularly in the South, was overcome through the efforts of authoritative government action. In the wake of busing, when white Southerners were given the opportunity to shop for schools by state laws, they opted largely to resegregate. The strongest evidence that history will repeat itself if people are given the opportunity to "shop" for public schools comes from magnet schools. Without specific mandates, magnet schools do not increase racial integration.

[R]esearch about the effects of magnets on desegregation has been clear: when not bolstered by mandates that ensure mixing, magnets have not increased racial integration. Moreover, because of the concentration of nonwhite students in inner cities, and the greater tendency of white urban students to attend private schools, minority students remain less likely to be with white students in public school magnets than they would be in private and religious schools.[43]

Disregarding the tendency toward resegregation that needs to be avoided, the ideal of parental choice does not play out ideally. Equity determined by parental choice assumes that all parents are fully informed of their choices and fully capable of acting in their child's best interests. This has been found not to be the case. For example, studies have shown that those parents most likely to choose were already actively involved in their child's education. Those children whose parents are less involved, likely because of economic constraints, will be less likely to enroll in choice programs.

Accountability

The privatization argument for accountability suggests that private schools are more accountable than public schools because public schools are unnaturally protected from failing. In the words of Alex Molnar,

> If you produce a product that people don't want, they don't buy your product and you fail. To them [advocates of privatization] that's accountability.[44]

Advocates of privatization also point to a more specific form of accountability resulting from privatization. Schools would no longer be accountable to the general public, only to their "customers." Parents and students are pictured as shopping for education, choosing the best schools, and rejecting the worst. As bad schools fail, demand for good schools at a cheap price forces good schools to open and provide for whomever needs schooling, whoever they are and wherever they live. This increased specificity of accountability, defined by allowing unfairly funded schools to fail, resembles the argument that private schooling is more democratic than public schooling.

Conservatives such as Helen Ladd often recognize the relationship between socioeconomic status and educational achievement that James Coleman's 1966 report demonstrated as the single most important relationship in determining educational achievement. For Ladd, this relationship points not to the need for initiatives for greater economic equality and cultural recognition but rather to the need for greater accountability and incentive programs. Ladd advocates methods that would allow teachers to factor out economic disadvantages in order to isolate students' achievement. Like Christopher T. Cross, Ladd understands education as a matter of enforcement. Low student achievement results from individual students who are lazy and do not want to learn. Such a conception of education derives from an economic model in which individuals only respond positively to a concrete incentive or reward and only are deterred from certain acts by explicit prohibitions such as punishment. Equity in this view refers to the creation of a strict meritocracy that factors out those disadvantages suffered by poor and nonwhite students. In other words, rather than considering how education can work to eliminate disadvantage, these authors seek to affirm disadvantage as a statistical variable in order to objectively measure hard work. Of course, these authors do not seek to factor racial or class privilege into their calculations.

Ladd's and Cross's market-based view of education as enforcement and coercion results in a hierarchical and antidemocratic understanding of accountability. Likewise, conservative charter-school champion Diane Ravitch insists that the virtue of charter schools is that they force public schools to improve by promoting competition.

> "As long as you have a system in which 90 percent of the kids are in the system and there's no interior reason to change, there will be this continual drift toward vacuity and illiteracy and social promotion," she observes. "But once you create these outlying organizations called charters, then the people inside the system will say, 'These people are getting public money; you've got to hold them accountable.' Then you produce a dynamic where even the people inside the system are demanding real standards."[45]

"The test for charter school reform is not those schools, but what happens in the rest of the system," writes privatization advocate John Chubb, who just happens to be a partner at the Edison Project, which is a for-profit company running charter schools in seven states.[46] The point here is that in these conservative arguments, competition and the market are viewed as natural remedies for an education system that suffers only from lack of discipline. These authors lack any sense of how historical inequalities and different levels of power and privilege shape present conditions.

Administrators enforce policy and curriculum implementation by threatening teachers with less job security and pay; teachers enforce mandated curricula by threatening students with bad grades or failure, or by expelling them. Accountability as enforcement puts standardized measurements of progress at the top of the educational agenda. As this happens, teaching becomes instrumentalized and knowledge trivialized. Freire has criticized this extensively as "banking education."

A more democratic form of education stresses meaningful learning that is attentive to the relationship between student experience, social structures, and the social production of knowledge. Learning must be meaningful in order for students to engage critically how knowledge is produced and distributed, to understand their own social position, and to connect knowledge to structures of power. The proliferation of more equal social relations depends in part upon teachers teaching for a freer and more equal society rather than for a narrow range of tests and skills. Of course, proficiency in basic skills is a desirable social goal—but to what end in a democracy? Education for democratic citizenry has very different implications than education for the economy. Giroux is worth quoting at length on this distinction.

> A debilitating logic is at work in the corporate model of teaching with its mandated curriculum, top-down teaching practices, and national tests to measure education standards. Infused with the drive toward standardized curricula and

teaching, "teachers and communities shorn of the capacity to use their own ideas, judgements, and initiative in matters of importance can't teach kids to do so." Such pedagogical approaches have little to do with teaching responsible citizenship because they redefine teaching less as an intellectual activity and more as a depoliticized, deskilled clerkship. . . . Moreover, within the standardized teaching models proffered by corporations, it becomes difficult to offer students the opportunity to think critically about the knowledge they gain, to appreciate the value of learning as more than the mastery of discrete bits of information, or to learn to use knowledge as a form of power to fight substantive injustices in a market-based society founded on deep inequalities. Finally, it is no small matter that the project that fuels privatization not only celebrates competitive, self-interested individuals attempting to further their own needs and aspirations, it also takes place within a discourse of decline, a jeremiad against public life, and in doing so actually undermines the role that public schools might play in keeping the experiences, hopes, and dreams of a democracy alive for each successive generation of students.[47]

Furthermore, the overreliance on standardized tests misleadingly suggests that the best schools are the richest and whitest ones.

[W]hen parents are left with standardized scores as the only readily available indicator of school performance, they are led almost inevitably to the conclusion that the "best" schools are those that have the fewest low-income and minority students. Expanding parental choice in an environment of such one-dimensional information will tend to reinforce tendencies toward racial and economic separation.[48]

In a broader social sense, accountability must refer to corporations being held accountable to the public for the power they wield. As Richard Grossman has advocated, one sure way of maintaining a corporate sphere subservient to the public well-being is by citizens invoking their rights to revoke corporate charters in the case of a corporation profiting at the expense of the commonweal.[49]

Educational privatization advocates also define accountability as bad schools closing. This view has no respect for the long-revered tradition of universal public education. Charter schools, performance contractors, and other private schools are subject to the bottom line and the decisions of absent owners. Public schools do not simply go out of business.

The operation and closing of the Juanita Virgil Academy was the most troublesome aspect of the first year of the Milwaukee Parental Choice Program. There are those who would argue that the failure of that school is to be expected in a

market system of education. Whether one believes that that expectation out-
weighs the fact that approximately 150 children essentially lost a year's education is a value issue that we cannot resolve. Whatever one's values are, the price
was high for those families involved.[50]

Public schools are also more accountable than private ones, in that they are
more subject to public oversight. As I have mentioned previously, countless
scandals involved business people bilking schools behind the curtain of corporate privacy. While privatizers have characterized public school administration as inefficient and encumbered with red tape, it is, in fact, a stable and
predictable bureaucratic structure that allows the public schools to provide
consistently better-quality education for less money than charters and performance contractors.

Democracy

The democracy argument for privatization holds that the market is more democratic than government. Chubb and Moe have elaborated the democracy argument for privatization most thoroughly. In their *Politics, Markets, and
America's Schools,* they charge that democracy in a heterogeneous and pluralistic society hurts education by allowing the will of the majority to be expressed through hierarchical regimes and bureaucratic modes of implementation. In such an environment teachers and administrators cannot develop the
teamwork, innovative spirit, and professionalism that effective education requires.[51] Most commonly, privatization is acclaimed as more democratic by
advocates of school choice. Here the shopping metaphorics of freedom of
choice merge with the democratic ideals of freedom of political participation.
This version of democracy understands individuals economically, primarily
as consumers concerned with getting the best deal. The privatization argument
from democracy contains a high degree of libertarian sentiment. Government
stands in the way of citizens' rights to choose goods and services. Consistent
with all of the other arguments for privatization, education is conceived as just
like any other good or service.

   There are three basic problems with this argument. First, Chubb and Moe
privilege bureaucratic structure over a political vision or the ideal of a democratic society. Thus, they transform political concerns into questions of efficiency. In this view democracy gets transformed from a social ideal to a
method or technique. This instrumentalized version of democracy wrongly
presumes that status quo relations of power are ideal. Second, market theory
conflates the freedom to shop around with genuine opportunity and is indifferent to existing inequalities. The market "is fundamentally indifferent to
existing inequalities in market power and the ways they shape people's actual

ability to choose."[52] Third, positing individuals as principally consuming subjects, market-based notions of democracy have no room for ideals of democratic equality or social transformation. The language of consuming subjects limits human agency to the act of consumption. Furthermore, a consumer-based sense of identity wrongly collapses social differences into a fictitious unity. Class differences, for example, become unintelligible or unspeakable to consuming subjects. In this view, we are united and equal in our potential as consumers. However, some are more equal than others. This limited notion of identity effaces the considerations of who has the power to control social decisions, who controls the means of material and cultural production and distribution, and who is excluded. These questions are fundamental to a genuine democracy.

NOTES

1. See Carol Ascher, Norm Fruchter, and Robert Berne, *Hard Lessons: Public Schools and Privatization* (New York: Twentieth Century Fund, 1996), which provides a historical overview of contemporary privatization endeavors and the paucity of evidence for any successes coming from experiments that have been conducted since the '70s.

2. See Ascher, Fruchter, and Berne, *Hard Lessons: Public Schools and Privatization*; see also Jeffrey Henig, *Rethinking School Choice* (Princeton: Princeton University Press, 1994), and Alex Molnar, *Giving Kids the Business* (Boulder: Westview, 1996), which comprehensively demonstrate the failures and dangers of privatization in these regards.

3. David Labaree, "An Unlovely Legacy," *Phi Delta Kappan* 75 no. 8 (April 1994): 592.

4. David Labaree, "Are Students 'Consumers'?" *Education Week* (17 September 1997): 38

5. Popular films such as *Dangerous Minds, The Substitute,* and *187,* as well as comedies that mock these films such as *High School High,* exemplify this racist portrayal and, in the case of these films, couple the suggestion of laziness with an intonation of urban nonwhite youth and youth culture as violent and dangerous.

6. The market metaphor of democracy defines democracy in market terms. As I discuss, John E. Chubb and Terry Moe, in *Politics, Markets, and America's Schools* (Washington, D.C.: Brookings Institute, 1990), offer the clearest and most noteworthy formulation of democracy reduced to capitalist management.

7. These metaphors can be found in both mass media news coverage of education and mainstream educational policy debates. For a liberal analysis of the language of the policy debates, see Henig's *Rethinking School Choice.* To see a more critical and elaborate discussion of the political role of language in policy debates and the role of language in the production of the cultural conditions for policy, see Henry A. Giroux, *Schooling and the Struggle for Public Life: Critical Pedagogy in the Modern*

Age (Minneapolis: University of Minnesota Press, 1988) and Henry A. Giroux, *Pedagogy and the Politics of Hope: Theory, Culture, and Schooling* (Boulder: Westview, 1997), and Aronowitz and Giroux, *Education Still Under Siege* (Westport: Bergin & Garvey, 1992).

8. Ascher, Fruchter, and Berne, *Hard Lessons: Public Schools and Privatization,* 14.

9. As cited in Ascher, Fruchter, and Berne, *Hard Lessons: Public Schools and Privatization,* 21–22.

10. Henig, *Rethinking School Choice,* 80.

11. See Aaron Gresson, *The Recovery of Race in America* (Minneapolis: University of Minnesota Press, 1995); Kobeena Mercer, *Welcome to the Jungle* (New York: Routledge, 1994); and Herman Gray, *Watching Race: Television and the Struggle for the Sign of Blackness* (Minneapolis: University of Minnesota Press, 1997) for discussions of the return of white supremacist sentiment as a part of the culture of Reaganism. All three situate the rise of white supremacy in relation to mass-mediated representations.

12. See Douglas Kellner's *Media Culture* or Aaron Gresson's *The Recovery of Race in America* for elaborate discussions of the recovery of white supremacy in mass-mediated representations in the '80s.

13. See Ruth Sidel, *Keeping Women and Children Last: America's War on the Poor* (New York: Penguin Books, 1996). See also Mark Zepezauer and Arthur Naiman, *Keep the Rich Off Welfare* (Tucson: Odonian Press, 1996), for a detailed comparison of federal budget expenditures on the military and social services.

14. When one considers federal expenditures on social services such as AFDC in relation to military spending, corporate welfare, and the billions of dollars that the Pentagon cannot account for in its balance sheets, it becomes apparent that it is not fundamentally economic scarcity driving initiatives such as the dismantling of welfare or the privatization of social security. Rather, what needs to be understood is that the struggle over social values is a part of a struggle over the very value of the social. Hyperindividualism links with the decline of social responsibility for individual well-being. Within this social logic of privatization, the well-being or abject status of individuals abstracts the situations individuals find themselves in from the social and historical conditions that produce these situations. Hence, the cause of poverty becomes poor people and the cause of crime becomes criminals. Responsibility and agency rendered radically individual yields a demand for individuals to justify their social usefulness. When public responsibility no longer becomes thinkable, the social logic goes like this: If poor people are poor, then they must be culpable for it. Yet public responsibility returns with a vengeance after the poor have been found guilty of poverty. And the public responsibility punishes the poor for their poverty in ways that redistribute funds to the wealthy. Workfare and the privatization of social services illustrate this phenomenon, as do the privatization and growth of the carceral industry.

15. Christian Parenti, *Lockdown America* (New York: Verso, 1999), 241.

16. Parenti, *Lockdown America,* 241.

17. The issue of the dangers to democracy of growing private control over public goods is taken up in Charles Derber, *Corporation Nation: How Corporations Are Taking Over Our Lives and What We Can Do about It* (New York: St. Martin's, 1998).

Robert Kuttner, *Everything for Sale* (New York: Knopf, 1996), and Richard L. Grossman and Frank T. Adams, *Taking Care of Business: Citizenship and the Charter of Incorporation* (Cambridge, Mass.: Charter, Ink. [a publication of the Program on Corporation, Law, and Democracy], 1995).

18. Ascher, Fruchter, and Berne, *Hard Lessons: Public Schools and Privatization,* 35.

19. The loss of local control that often accompanies privatization should not serve as an argument for local control in the form of vouchers. On the contrary, authoritative government action is also nonlocal, yet it is superior in that it is justified on ethical and political grounds of democratic equality, not private profit.

20. Henig, *Rethinking School Choice,* xiii.

21. *A Nation at Risk.*

22. Thomas Toch, *In the Name of Excellence* (New York: Oxford University Press, 1991), 17.

23. Molnar, *Giving Kids the Business,* 1.

24. Molnar, *Giving Kids the Business,* 18.

25. Molnar, *Giving Kids the Business,* 18.

26. Molnar, *Giving Kids the Business,* 6.

27. Joseph P. Viteritti, "Stacking the Deck for the Poor: The New Politics of School Choice," *The Brookings Review* 14, no. 3 (Summer 1996): 12.

28. Molnar, *Giving Kids the Business,* 7.

29. "Popular Economics Workshop of the Western Pennsylvania Living Wage Campaign," Bureau of the Census, Department of Commerce.

30. Molnar, *Giving Kids the Business,* 2.

31. Henig, *Rethinking School Choice,* 27.

32. Berliner, *The Manufactured Crisis* (New York: Longman, 1995), 634.

33. Ascher, Fruchter, and Berne, *Hard Lessons: Public Schools and Privatization,* 85.

34. Ascher, Fruchter, and Berne, *Hard Lessons: Public Schools and Privatization,* 85.

35. Laurence Ogle and Patricia Dabbs, "Good News, Bad News: Does Media Coverage of the Schools Promote Scattershot Remedies?" *Education Week* (13 March 1996): 46.

36. Henig, *Rethinking School Choice,* 31–32.

37. Henig, *Rethinking School Choice,* 51–52.

38. Ascher, Fruchter, and Berne, *Hard Lessons: Public Schools and Privatization,* 35.

39. Ascher, Fruchter, and Berne, *Hard Lessons: Public Schools and Privatization,* 35.

40. Chester Finn, Louann Bierlein, and Manno Bruno, "Finding the Right Fit: America's Charter Schools Get Started," *The Brookings Review* 14, no. 3 (Summer 1996): 19.

41. James Traub, "In Theory: A School of Your Own," *New York Times,* 4 April 1999.

42. Pedro A. Noguera, "More Democracy Not Less: Confronting the Challenge of Privatization in Public Education," *Journal of Negro Education* 63, no. 2 (1994): 238.

43. Ascher, Fruchter, and Berne, *Hard Lessons: Public Schools and Privatization,* 18.

44. Molnar, *Giving Kids the Business,* 138.

45. Traub, "In Theory: A School of Your Own."

46. Traub, "In Theory: A School of Your Own."

47. Giroux, "Corporate Culture," 36–37.

48. Henig, *Rethinking School Choice,* 214.

49. Grossman and Adams, *Taking Care of Business.*

50. Ascher, Fruchter, and Berne, *Hard Lessons: Public Schools and Privatization,* 73.

51. Henig, *Rethinking School Choice,* 9.

52. Henig, *Rethinking School Choice,* 192.

2

Nothing Left to Choose: Education, Democracy, and School Choice

THE LANGUAGE OF CHOICE

The vast corpus of literature on the subject of school choice offers readers an endless array of justifications for why school choice promises educational salvation, and an equally endless array offers warnings about the hazards of school choice. I mention this not to imply that these arguments somehow cancel each other out, rendering a generally innocuous phenomenon with some good aspects and some bad. Nor do I mention the school choice debate as an entree into a review of the literature followed by a taking of sides—though warnings are in order and will arise in the course of this chapter. The positive-sounding term *school choice* cannot be viewed as "*a* phenomenon" at all. In fact, the singular term has misleadingly come to encapsulate a number of contradictory and conflicting reform visions. For example, government controlled choice programs aimed at remedying long-standing racial inequality are fundamentally equity-based, typically with a liberal democratic vision, while market-based choice initiatives are concerned principally with fiscal profit for investors or with social efficiency defined in economic rather than democratic terms. In the context of the current educational reform debates, placing radically different programs under the same rubric risks forwarding one particular version of school choice, namely market-based choice, at the expense of careful consideration of the competing versions and their underlying social visions. This is because the current educational reform debates have come to be monopolized by the language and logic of the market.

Much more is at stake in the school choice debate than the establishment of academic delineations. The struggle over school choice reflects a broader struggle over the social function of schooling and, in an even more overarching

33

sense, the role of schooling in a society committed to democracy. The choice debates concern larger ethical and political questions. In light of a growing economic rationalism in all spheres, educators must be concerned with the dangers of putting the market ahead of human concerns, basic rights, and cultural and material equity. The dangers of the market-based view of society include mistaking corporate health for the well-being of the bulk of the population.

As cities and states offer public funds to woo massive corporations to their locales for the promise of a few part-time jobs with no benefits, one must recognize that the apparent subjection of the state to the private sphere has come, in part, as the result of a shift in common sense and conventional wisdom. The assumption that corporate well-being supersedes or grants the well-being of citizens has taken hold in popular culture and in mass media. For example, the framing of citizens as consumers in mass media redefines the democratic subject as a consuming subject primarily concerned with the individual concerns of bargains and investments and less concerned with the common good. As identity and language become redefined in corporate terms, the democratic tradition of universal care, equity, and concern with the social becomes superfluous. This can be witnessed in the way that education debates have become "monopolized" by the market terms of efficiency, competition, quality, and management. Students are characterized as clients and teachers as service workers. The market logic goes so far as to suggest that the solution to poor public schools is to let them fail just like noncompetitive businesses.

The insidious results of this thinking can be seen in the rise of school choice programs. For example, New Jersey has launched a test in which ten school districts will accept, tuition-free, students from other districts in the state.

> The districts in the pilot program will receive payments from the state for each incoming student. Those losing the students will continue to receive state aid for each one, but that figure would be reduced by 25 percent in the first year, 50 percent in the second year, and finally by 75 percent. State officials have little expectation that parents in such communities as Princeton or Summit, with their excellent schools, will decide to transfer to one of the 10 districts in the program. The hope is that each of the 10, which will be closely monitored by the state, will work to come up with unique programs to attract students who need a new educational setting. . . . "We're just trying to become a part of the movement to offer students more choices."[1]

In other words, public money is being transferred from poor districts into rich districts. This upward redistribution of resources is being called "choice."

However, it really demonstrates the increasing limitation of choice for poorer districts in the state as they are defunded.

Beyond the fact that the market has no heart, the market lacks ethical and political bounds that put human interests ahead of profit. Market logic did not prevent thousands of German corporations from using concentration camp labor during World War II. Nor has it provided any reason not to exploit child labor today, as corporate Goliaths Nike, the Gap, and Disney do in Indonesia. The market cannot be relied upon to provide for most citizens. Increasing reliance on corporations to serve the common good and mistaken belief in the autonomy of the economy increase the possibilities of a material and ideological war against the least fortunate members of society. The economic efficiency model perpetuates the upward redistribution of wealth and the continually shrinking real wage.[2] As more and more people have less and less, elites in control of the bulk of the wealth and in control of the cultural ideological machinery, including mass media, will be forced to blame others for the souring of social life. Domestically, those with the least ability to respond effectively to the scapegoating are most likely to be blamed for social ills. This means poor, nonwhite, and immigrant populations become increasingly vulnerable to popular scorn, new legislation directed against them, and a further loss of social services to which they should be entitled. The hoarding of wealth and power by elites also increases the likelihood of the creation of newly designated foreign and domestic enemies to scapegoat for the decreasing standard of living experienced by most citizens.

Beyond education, the positive-sounding language of choice conspires to redefine public services as private commodities. The privatization of public utilities such as electricity has overtaken many cities. These schemes, which are designed to increase corporate profits, are publicly justified as being in the interest of "the consumer." However, one of the fundamental rules of economics is "there is no such thing as a free lunch." When the increased competition for electricity carriers forces deliverers to lay off workers, to skimp on quality, or to employ dangerous or environmentally destructive cost-saving techniques, the supposed minimal cost savings for consumers will be paid for by a decrease in working conditions for electricity workers, damage to nature, and other social costs. Likewise, when education becomes privatized through the use of market-based choice or other voucher schemes, there are other social costs such as a loss of stable, predictable administration; highly uneven quality between districts; noneducators running schools; or racial resegregation.[3]

Some of these competing versions of school choice include: government-controlled choice, psychologically based choice, communal value–based choice, community power–based nonmarket choice, and the aforementioned market-based choice. In what follows I sketch a picture of these various school choice platforms in order to extract their best elements. Next I draw together these elements to propose the necessary components of a democratic form of school choice. Finally, I look to notions of critical pedagogy and radical democracy to refine a version of school choice that exceeds current conceptions of choice in the scope of social, cultural, and economic equality.

VERSIONS OF SCHOOL CHOICE

Market-Based Choice

School choice originates, in a policy sense, in modern times with Milton Friedman's vouchers proposal of the '50s that appeared in book form as part of *Capitalism and Freedom* in 1962.[4] Friedman's libertarian sentiments, which first foreshadowed and then became a basis for the Reagan revolution, posit government as a threat to individual freedom. Friedman recommends minimal government involvement in most social spheres and instead advocates private delivery of goods and services on the assumption that the competition of the market creates inherent efficiencies that public entities are incapable of equaling. While Friedman recognized that a role of education is the making of democratic citizenry, he proposed that government be relieved of its role as direct provider of education. Rather, in his view, the government should provide vouchers and impose certain minimum standards on private schools through licensing.

Friedman's libertarian proposals were initially at odds with the spirit of the times. He specifically attacks Kennedy's call, "ask not what your country can do for you; ask what you can do for your country," claiming that both parts of this statement are coercive and paternalistic. It would take years of upward material redistribution, corporate cultural pedagogy, shifting political and social climates, and a deliberately constructed coalition for Friedman's ideas to have their current force and acceptability as market-based choice.

Friedman, and market-based choice more generally, conceives of individuals as rational actors in a social system that offers opportunities for all who are capable and skilled at taking advantage of them. Individuals are free when not constrained by intrusive forces. Because they are free, individuals will pursue their own interests to the fullest extent of their abilities. Government authority is only useful as it protects some individuals from the potentially harmful actions of others. Government authority is, hence, inherently authoritarian and yet at times a necessary evil. The market, in Friedman's view, serves as the medium through which individuals express their needs and desires. Thus, in Friedman's world, the market becomes more than the place where business is transacted. It becomes a symbol of freedom, both in terms of individual autonomy and self-expression, and socially as the medium of the individual's free pursuit of wealth and interest.

In individual terms, this view of the market as liberating panacea contradicts the day-to-day experience of most people in the marketplace. I think that aside from the momentary thrill of rare luxury purchases, very few people feel liberated by most of the purchases they make. The market produces bad feelings—feelings of lack, that one never has enough, feelings of doubt, "Have I been cheated?" and feelings of being bombarded by endless sell-jobs. If it were not for the government protecting citizens from corporate greed, these bad feelings would more commonly include, "Am I being poisoned by this tubercular beef?" and the actual feelings of being poisoned.[5]

In addition to being at odds with most people's experience of the market, Friedman's celebration of the market presumes that the market is a "level playing field" on which individuals pursue their interests to the best of their ability. Friedman fails to realize that America's pluralistic environment breeds different social and cultural values. His meritocratic ideal treats culture as singular and unified. In fact, when culture is thought of severally, in terms of cultures, it becomes apparent that Friedman's competitive and meritocratic ideal assumes that the culture with the most power—white, male culture—is the only culture. In other words, the "level playing field" presupposed by advocates of market-based school choice is a farce. The problem is not that African Americans, women, and other groups without access to equal competition fail to promote the skills necessary to compete. Rather, historical oppressions have resulted in the formation of institutions structured in inequality and a culture in which racism and sexism are endemic rather than anomalous.[6] America needs radical change in the form of radically egalitarian structures to replace capitalism, patriarchy, and white supremacy. Education must be a part of this radical transformation rather than the route to a supposed meritocracy in a society structured by brutal, oppressive, and hierarchical social relations.

The "level playing field" idealized by free market celebrants is actually slanted uphill two ways: first, nondominant groups are excluded from the institutions that favor dominant groups and second, dominant groups are taught that their institutions are universally inclusive. Hence, not only are nonwhites, women, the poor, and other subjugated groups prevented from participation in the (not so free) market in a material sense, due to a society structured in inequality, but moreover, the denial of privilege on the part of privileged people then stigmatizes those groups that have been actively excluded. This stigmatization of the oppressed then functions to justify their continued exclusion and simultaneously allows the privileged to deny their privileged status based on the alleged inadequacies of the oppressed. This happens precisely because dominant cultures become neutralized or "invisiblized" and become conflated with culture itself. The issues surrounding market-based choice do not merely concern economic struggle.

In fact, it is impossible to talk about school choice apart from the history of racism, with which it is inextricably linked. In practice, school choice originated in the late '60s as a racist tactic employed by Southern school districts to counter federally initiated desegregation measures such as busing. Following the initiatives of the civil rights movement, the federal government took decisive action to attempt to remedy a separate and highly unequal mode of schooling. Southern states such as Virginia, Mississippi, Alabama, and Georgia moved to flout federal laws by creating state and local laws allowing for school choice. Essentially, these local laws gave the families of white students the ability to still receive public funding for schools that would continue to exclude nonwhites. Lengthy court battles eventually found these local laws to be unconstitutional. However, their implementation allowed legally sanctioned segregation for years beyond the official end of segregated schooling.

Friedman was writing before the civil rights movement. Separate public facilities for whites and nonwhites were law in the South. Northern racism was just slightly less overt but equally insidious. De facto apartheid was the norm. Years of strong government intervention have achieved integration, universal education, and a significant rise in high school graduation rates. Authoritative government affirmative action programs also expanded college attendance, transforming what was prior to civil rights an elite white institution into a more multicultural yet not fully representative system.

Market-based choice that views the government as essentially oppressive and views individuals as equal competitors fails to account for the important role of government in protecting individuals and groups from the legacy of historically racial, ethnic, or gendered market-based oppressions such as slavery, segregation, and disenfranchisement.[7] There is a certain absurdity in advocating market solutions for market-induced problems. For example, the failings of many nonwhite public schools owe their existence in large part to the chronic underfunding of these schools by corporate de-taxation and a market-based way of funding local schools using the local tax base.

Market-based choice suggests that freedom derives from the freedom to shop for education.

"It's very simple," said David Anthony, the president of the Hoboken school district. "How many choices can you offer a child to go to school? It's like college. If you do well, you can go to Harvard. If you don't do as well, there are a lot of other choices."[8]

The shopping metaphor wrongly implies a meritocratic outcome to market-based choice. In Anthony's praise of choice, he neglects to mention that Harvard attendance is limited to those who can afford it. The suggestion that admission depends upon natural ability conflates affluence and intelligence. Anthony, of course, also assumes that the knowledge required for entrance to Harvard is value-neutral and does not represent particular class, gender, and racial values, perspectives, and histories. Choices are not only constrained by economic means but by what French sociologist Pierre Bourdieu has termed *cultural capital*—that is, the level of embodied and possessed socially valued and legitimated knowledge.

The logic of the shopping metaphor also says, "All parents can shop for the best education for their children." The best shoppers get the best bargains. In reality, parental decisions are not limited to choosing the best school. The geography of the school, the cultural composition of the school, as well as many other factors play a part in parental governance. Furthermore, it would be wrong to assume that all parents are capable of choosing the best schools for their children. Many factors play into choices, such as the desire of nonwhite parents to keep their children in the community or the desire of white racist parents to keep their children away from nonwhites. Historically, without strong government intervention choice has been a prescription for increased racial segregation and the maintenance of an apartheid-like structure of schooling.

This being the case, why should children suffer because their parents make the "wrong" choice? Most important, the schools targeted for school choice are those public schools that are currently underfunded and are largely working class and nonwhite. Providing a few thousand dollars per student in vouchers for poor families to choose among underfunded schools does not solve the fundamental problem of a public school system that is structured unequally. White suburban children receive several times more money and generally receive excellent public education. They are seldom subjected to market-based school choice plans. This points to the fact that educational reform should be expanding the successes of public education for all students rather than robbing poor and nonwhite students of the same educational opportunities afforded the wealthiest public school students. In fact, choice needs to be understood as a redistribution of choice.

The rhetoric of educational choice emphasizes individual liberty, breaking down the walls that constrain us. One man's liberty, however, can be another man's corral. When we move from abstraction to policy, it becomes apparent that almost every workable plan entails, first of all, a *redistribution* of choice. . . . The winners and losers are not preordained. Lower-income groups currently locked in ghetto public schools would benefit under some conceivable choice schemes; under other arrangements the principal beneficiaries would be middle and upper income families given the freedom to redirect personal funds now dedicated to private school tuition. Given economic and educational disparities, both among families and across school districts, there is a serious risk, of course, that choice-in-practice will expand the opportunities of those already advantaged, at the ultimate cost of limiting opportunities for those greatest in need.[9]

Market-based choice is one of the schemes that risk benefiting those who are already advantaged under the current system at the expense of those who are already losing.

Because market-based choice is not situated in a broader social ideal concerned with the common good, it disconnects schooling from questions of the purpose of schooling in a democratic society. Consequently, it risks perpetuating or worsening current social inequalities. In fact, in the case of market-based choice, the term *reform* is a misnomer. Market-based choice should be understood as a dismantling of the democratic ideal of universal public schooling, as a redistribution of authority and control from the public to private investors, and as the redistribution of choice. Thought of in terms of the individual, market-based choice mistakenly assumes full autonomy and envisions individuals wrenched from the constraints of social contexts. In societal terms, market-based choice fails to comprehend the need for a common good, misunderstands government authority as inevitably authoritarian, presumes a monoculture, and wrongly supposes that culture is a "level playing field." Because market-based choice fails to comprehend difference beyond different markets, it treats pluralism as a matter of niche marketing. Within this view there is no room for taking seriously issues of power-sharing by different groups, histories of oppression and inequality that inform the present, or the inevitability of political struggle to any social arrangement. Hence, I reject market-based school choice for its inability to recognize some essential elements of democracy—namely, pluralism, a strong public sphere, equitable distribution of resources, and a market in the service of the public rather than a public sphere in the service of private interests.

Psychological Choice

Some critics of market-based choice have based their claims in the individual terms of psychology. John E. Coons and Stephen D. Sugarman emphasize choice as a cognitive concept that, they argue, should be understood as a tool for the intellectual and moral development of children. They take issue with economists for elevating the household into the primary unit for economic decision making. They argue that this takes too much for granted the premise that the family is "a competent agent for the child."[10] While this notion of choice does not propose a specific form of school reform, psychologically based choice offers another perspective from which to criticize market-based choice and provides a way of thinking about the necessary elements of a positive conception of choice.

What are the implications of framing choice in individual terms as a tool for the intellectual and moral development of children? Choice should always be thought of as a tool. However, choice is a tool that needs to be situated in a social and political framework.

> Individual choice is a value worth protecting; it can also be a useful tool in the collective arsenal. But its effectiveness in addressing social problems depends on its being used in the context of confident and legitimate government authority, not as an alternative to such authority. Democratic procedures and institutions have a central role to play in building the deeper and broader-based coalition that is needed if attention to education is to be serious and sustained. Rather than substituting one proposed panacea—choice—with another . . . what is needed [asks Henig] to mobilize such a receptive coalition. Part of the answer, happily, leads us to a richer conception of education: education not just as one among many services that government may provide, but as one of the most important ways in which democracies can create the conditions for their own vitality and growth.[11]

While Henig is correct in his assertion that choice needs to be thought of as a tool for democratic governance, he offers little in the way of a critique of actually existing liberal democracy, nor does he propose that the role of schooling include social transformation to a better formulation of political principles than those built into liberal democracy. Like Henig, Henry A. Giroux recognizes that choice needs to be understood as a tool and needs to be situated within a political framework. However, Giroux looks to the political theory of radical democracy as proposed by Laclau and Mouffe as an alternative political referent to democratic liberalism.[12] I discuss the advantages of radical democracy over liberal democracy further on. Coons and Sugarman are correct to criticize market-based choice for assuming that the family is a "competent agent for the child." However, Coons and Sugarman err in suggesting a highly individualized notion of choice defined in developmental terms.

Individual choices are constrained by the social field, by the individual's positionality, and by such factors as the race, class, religion, and gender of the individual. In short, to talk about choice in a way that divorces it from social relations renders a philosophically abstract metaphysical conception of choice. Of course, this universalizing sense of choice comes from particular traditions, particular positions, with their own sets of values. Choice as described by Coons and Sugarman comes out of a Cartesian-Kantian tradition that imagines the individual as fully autonomous and rationally directed and presumes "neutral" political principles to which any "rational" individual should adhere. Coons and Sugarman's advocacy of children's development of intellectual and moral autonomy through an individualized sense of choice will inevitably result in a philosophically liberal effacement of politics and power and a refusal to recognize difference as constitutive of the social.

Psychological choice makes the same mistake as market-based choice in presuming a singular culture. This presumption allows proponents to believe that all individuals have the same opportunities to exercise their capacity for choice. In the case of both, this erases the social struggle over values, meaning, and history that is woven through the social field. Such an erasure of struggle serves dominant interests by neutralizing and naturalizing them and then subjecting the nondominant to this standard.

One important lesson that can be gleaned from psychological choice is that choice needs to be understood as a tool but as a tool for furthering democratic ends, not as an end in itself or as a tool merely for individual edification. Second, choice needs to be understood in social contexts, not merely individual or psychological terms. When conceived in strictly individual terms, choice becomes depoliticized and, hence, becomes complicitous in reproducing and invisiblizing structures of inequality.

Communal Value–Based Choice

Both of the versions of choice discussed so far—market-based choice and psychological choice—treat culture as singular and hence fail to respect the pluralism and diversity integral to genuine democracy. Communal value–based choice concerns precisely what the other two lack. Communal value–based choice principally concerns pluralism and cultural recognition by groups who have been historically misrecognized. By cultural recognition, I mean what philosopher Charles Taylor has described in his important essay "The Politics of Recognition." Misrecognition, or nonrecognition,

> can be a form of oppression, imprisoning someone in a false, distorted, reduced mode of being. Beyond simple lack of respect, it can inflict a grievous wound, saddling people with crippling self-hatred. Due recognition is not just a courtesy but a vital human need.[13]

Communal value–based choice proponents embrace school choice plans with individual group interests as their principal concern. In light of historical oppressions, some groups reject a relation between their group and the broader society. For example, citing the failure of public schooling to have achieved racially equitable education, black nationalists place the group interests of African Americans above the common good. Hence, school choice, even market-based school choice, becomes a possible route to the furthering of the groups' interests.

Polly Williams has been one of the most outspoken advocates of market-based school choice on the grounds that the interests of African Americans have not been served by public schooling. Fiscal conservatives have embraced some black nationalists such as Williams because the privatization/antipublic goals of conservatives coincide with the communal value/antipublic goals of activists and other leaders who seek to advance their group in the words of black Republican Alan Keyes, "by any means necessary." Keyes's words reiterate yet reinvent Malcolm X's message about the need for radical struggle. Yet Malcolm X did not quite have in mind the strategy of fighting inequity by joining the fiscal conservatives in the Republican Party. The cultural separatism of communal value–based choice shares with market-based choice a balkanizing tendency that elides the need for a strong sense of the common good.

Proponents of communal value–based choice fail to see the extent to which capitalism has been instrumental in forming and perpetuating the racist institutions to which these proponents are subject. For example, the very invention of race as a concept and category emerged to justify the economic pursuits—the business of slavery—of a ruling class of white Europeans.[14] Since the end of slavery, race has been a very useful "divide and conquer" strategy on the part of an economic ruling class to redirect mass resentment. Working-class whites have largely been taught to blame nonwhites and immigrants rather than the ruling class for unemployment, poor working conditions, and job competition.

In terms of more recent history, the Reagan/Bush/Clinton era has been characterized by a steady upward redistribution of wealth and a steadily declining real wage.[15] Corporations have not accepted the blame for this unfair redistribution, yet racist ideologies embodied in mass-mediated representations have worked to shift the blame onto nonwhites, immigrants, and other marginalized groups, in a sense, selling blame as entertainment.[16] The success of this ideological war has had a vicious material aftermath, including the transformation of African-American men into commodities in the booming carceral industry. More generally, communal value–based choice in its hyperpluralism can yield antipluralist effects. In lending credibility to market-based choice, communal value–based choice can result in the strengthening of a culturally homogenizing, capitalist-justified form of education. The imperatives of the market and the bottom line can redefine difference in market and profit terms and erase a more meaningful definition of difference that remains connected with history and group struggle. For example, power within a market-based model becomes understood in a "might makes right" way rather than in a democratic fashion.

The extreme pluralism of communal value–based choice has no way of connecting the struggles of a single group to a larger political and ethical framework or overarching set of principles. An incidental result of this is the increased power of dominant groups whose interests are ultimately at odds with most members of the communal value–based group. In sharing with market-based choice a willingness for radical reform and a willingness to abandon the public or any sense of the broader common good, communal value–based choice rushes into an unholy alliance with a market reform vision ultimately unconcerned with the principal pluralistic aims of the communal vision. Unfortunately, the vast divide between these two visions will only become manifest *after* public schooling has been weakened further by the success of market-based reform.

Finally, by virtue of its extreme pluralism, communal value–based choice relies upon a politics of authenticity in which difference within groups cannot be theorized. Hence, African Americans, for example, become essentialized, totalized, and singularized. This renders difficult an understanding of the internalization of white supremacy expressed through skin tone hierarchies within the African-American community. Communal value–based choice also views the individual in authentic terms. This leaves no way to explain the nonalignment of identity and ideology. For example, it cannot explain how an African-American man such as Alan Keyes can join the Republican Party, which often espouses racist policies and officially denies and distorts the history of oppression of African Americans.

Liberal Redistributive Voucher Plans

Early in the history of school choice, liberals were seeing the potential of school choice as a tool for promoting greater equity. In 1966 former *New Republic* education editor Christopher Jencks worked with the U.S. Office of Economic Opportunity to design a policy experiment. The OEO, which was staffed by proponents of community action and Lyndon Johnson's War on Poverty, was more interested in the potential of vouchers to redistribute opportunity to benefit minorities and the poor. Jencks's voucher proposal differed from Friedman's markedly. For Friedman, wealthier individuals would be able to subsidize their voucher amount and individual school districts would be able to raise the voucher amount, thus increasing per-pupil spending over less wealthy districts with weaker property tax bases. Jencks and other liberals, including then Harvard Graduate School of Education dean Theodore Sizer, envisioned a much more equitably based voucher system. Sizer favored vouchers only if they were structured "to discriminate in favor of poor children" and warned that "a voucher plan for all children (not just poor children) that replaced some existing sources of public aid would cripple the public schools and would give excessive power to middle-class parents."[17]

For Jencks, voucher schools would have to accept half of their students randomly and accept each voucher as full payment to decrease racial, ethnic, and wealth-based discrimination. In addition, schools would be offered "compensatory payments" as a way of inducing them to accept lower-income students. Like Sizer, Jencks expressed the sentiment that a voucher system must pursue increased equity for poorer students and, like Sizer, he stressed that the failure to do so would "be worse than no voucher system at all."

Though communal value–based choice offers a strong sense of pluralism, like market-based and psychological choice, it lacks a sense of the common good. Liberal vouchers are the first form of choice that both concerns pluralistic ideals and has a strong sense of the common good. Liberal voucher plans offer a welfare justification for a progressive form of school choice concerned with economic equity along cultural, racial, and ethnic lines. As such, liberal vouchers far exceed the other versions of school choice thus examined. However, even this progressive version of choice has certain severe problems. It is toward these problems that I now turn. I must mention first that liberal voucher plans have historically offered the best hope for a democratic version of school choice. One question I will revisit is whether school choice can ever be reconciled with genuine democracy.

The first major problem with liberal voucher plans is that while they do concern pluralism, they do not take seriously power sharing by different groups. Their overreliance on a strong sense of the common good renders an inability to comprehend such issues as who has the power to set the economic and cultural agendas. Liberal voucher plans presuppose that the system is fundamentally fair yet has some kinks that need to be worked out. In other words, liberal voucher plans seek to redress inequalities but not address or change the underlying structures that produce these inequalities. Namely, institutions based in capitalism, racism, patriarchy, and heterosexism need to be replaced with more egalitarian structures that facilitate power sharing, not merely recognition of difference expressed through tokenism or the willingness to include the excluded in dominant institutions.

New institutions are in order. Political theorist Nancy Fraser offers a helpful matrix for distinguishing liberal "affirmative" remedies from the radical transformations necessary for a society structured in equality. As Fraser points out, affirmative economic remedies, such as the liberal welfare state solution to poverty, result in the stigmatization of the very cultural groups targeted for help. By merging socialist economics with deconstructive cultural theory, Fraser offers a radical solution concerned with restructuring social relations. Contrary to the liberal view, for Fraser, economics (both in form and in its portrayal) is no longer defined by the interests of capital and the ruling class, and cultural politics does not remain organized around seemingly static group differences such as whiteness and blackness but rather around the process of deconstructing seemingly fixed categories.

Another problem with liberal voucher plans is that even well-intentioned liberal voucher school choice can evolve into a privatization scheme at odds with the original intent. This possibility was recognized early in the history of school choice. In response to the OEO experiment plans, unions and teachers' associations banded together and fought what they viewed as an inevitable attack on teachers' work. The American Federation of Teachers, the National Education Association, the National Association of Elementary School Principals, and the American Association of School Administrators, recognizing the implications of the voucher experiments, told a congressional committee that pursuit of the experiment meant that the "original purpose of OEO—assistance to the poor—has been redirected into an ill-conceived attempt to reprivatize our social services."[18] These prescient sentiments were in fact well reasoned. As I discuss in chapter 1, it was the very possibility of the slippage from public school choice to privatization that Ronald Reagan seized upon in the beginning of his second term that began the enacted choice movement. Reagan succeeded in attributing to choice the success of the government-mandated magnet schools. He isolated choice from the strong government authority that had successfully used it and claimed that the market would be even better at promoting choice. In fact, the magnet schools were put in place by authoritative government action as an attempt at remedying racist inequities. Through rhetorical sleight of hand, Reagan suggested that the high quality of the magnet schools was a result of choice and that public school choice is best facilitated by increased competition. Reagan successfully unlinked choice from equity and relinked it to market ideals of efficiency and competition. This highly duplicitous move wrongly suggested that the success of choice was due to market forces rather than government forces, that there was popular support for market-based choice, and that the magnet schools were always about efficiency, not equity. This example shows several things: (1) well-intentioned equity-based choice is not immune from political struggle and from being redefined in antidemocratic ways; (2) words are powerful tools in shaping public opinion and policy; (3) the language of choice as a metaphor lends itself to a market-based vision for schooling; and (4) language matters tremendously in the political struggle over education.

Community Power–Based Nonmarket Choice

Community power–based nonmarket choice is the first version mentioned so far that concerns pluralism and yet does not put group interest above the common good or, like liberal vouchers, put the common good ahead of power-sharing. Henig offers an explanation of community power–based nonmarket choice.

> The community-power rationale for expanding educational choice sees schools as rooted in interest-group theories of politics. Communities—linked by race and class, and forced into spatial patterns by discrimination and economic inequities—represent legitimate units of political mobilization. Schools are an important prize in the battle among communities striving to maximize their resources and status. But schools are more than a trophy; they are an important resource in the ongoing battle. Reliable and sustainable mobilization demands a shared identity, a sense of political efficacy, and experience in exercising power. Schools can augment a community's stock in these valuable commodities by reinforcing and transmitting local values, by providing skills along with opportunities to exercise them in ways that build self-confidence, and by giving students and parents a local arena in which they can be drawn into the collective experience of democratic control. . . . The penetration of schools by higher levels of authority potentially undermines these conditions, however, by imposing the norms of the dominant groups, by deemphasizing or belittling racial and class-specific heroes and history, by maintaining an atmosphere of reduced expectations, and by preempting positions of authority.[19]

The community-power view of choice offers clear advantages over the other views of choice thus discussed. Understanding society in terms of agonistic interest groups has several advantages over communal value–based choice. First, communal value–based choice in the liberal tradition lacks a sense of the political, whereas community-power choice has a strong sense of the inevitability of conflict constitutive of any social arrangement. While community power–based choice both is pluralistic and views the social agonistically, we can refine this vision by complementing it with the insights of the political theory of radical democracy, which recognizes the decenteredness of both identity and the social. As we will see, the anti-essentialism of radical democracy, as well as its attention to power sharing and its centrality of politics, offers a more radical theory of choice as a democratic tool and one less apt to slippage into use for market ends. As well, if school choice must be thought of as a tool for democratization, then radical democracy offers a more comprehensive picture of democracy than liberal democracy, from which all of the previously discussed theories stem.

Radical Democracy

In *The Return of the Political,* Chantal Mouffe explains a central deficit of liberal democracy—what she terms "the Political." The Political refers to the inevitability of conflict central to any political configuration. Drawing on the political philosophy of Carl Schmitt, Mouffe points to the friend/enemy grouping, which forms the basis of politics, to suggest that society needs to be understood as *constituted* by incompatibility and difference. Recognizing the inherently conflictive nature of society calls for the formulation of political principles that draw on political liberalism's tradition of individual rights and the communitarian tradition's insistence on the common good. Political liberalism refers to the political philosophy of liberal thought, which includes both American conservatism and American liberalism. Both are firmly within the liberal tradition. Political liberalism values individual rights over common goods, understands the individual in the Kantian tradition as fully autonomous and rationally directed, and presumes "neutral" political principles to which any "rational" individual should adhere. As such, liberal democracy, in Mouffe's words, is incapable of comprehending the political. She writes,

> Once we accept the necessity of the political and the impossibility of a world without antagonism, what needs to be envisaged is how it is possible under those conditions to create or maintain a pluralistic democratic order.[20]

Liberal democracy's inability to see conflict as constitutive and its insistence upon rational consensus to a so-called neutral common good leave it unable to make sense of the new alignments following the end of communism. During the Cold War, liberal democracy was defined in opposition to totalitarianism. The end of the Cold War brought on an identity crisis for the West, with the resultant scramble to re-establish the friend/enemy frontiers. Mouffe elaborates,

> In the West, it is the very identity of democracy which is at stake, in so far as it has depended to a large extent on the existence of the Communist "other" that

constituted its negation. Now that the enemy has been defeated, the meaning of democracy itself has become blurred and needs to be redefined by the creation of a new frontier. This is much more difficult for the moderate right and for the left than for the radical right. For the latter has already found its enemy. It is provided by the "enemy within," the immigrants, which are presented by the different movement of the extreme right as a threat to the cultural identity and national sovereignty of the "true" Europeans. I submit that the growth of the extreme right in several countries in Europe can only be understood in the context of the deep crisis of political identity that confronts liberal democracy following the loss of the traditional landmarks of politics. It is linked to the necessity of redrawing the political frontier between friend and enemy.[21]

Specifically in the American context, we can see the crisis of political identity as it has been playing out on a variety of fronts. The rise of right-wing radicalism in the United States has not only fired up anti-immigrant sentiment, as expressed in the denial of government aid to legal immigrants and in new laws in California that even moderates have labeled racist, but also in widespread right-wing terrorism. The Oklahoma bombing of a federal building, the torching of black churches in the South, and the increasing visibility of white supremacist militia groups and the Klan signify shifted alliances. For the far right in the United States, the communist threat has been largely replaced by new enemies within: the U.S. government, the "liberal" media, Arabs, Jews, blacks, and other nonwhites. Equally revealing of the crisis of liberal democracy is the sheer inability of the mainstream news media to comprehend this startling trend. The Timothy McVeigh bombing and trial coverage framed the bombing as the calculated actions of a lone evil man. None of the coverage explored McVeigh's proclamations of being a right-wing revolutionary, nor, finally and most significantly, did it raise the critical question of the meaning of the rise of right-wing radicalism and other types of fundamentalism at the current historical juncture.

Far from being peripheral to education, critically comprehending these events and their greater political implications is central to establishing the democratic prerequisites for a new theory of school choice. Education needs to be understood as part of a larger commitment to rethinking democracy in light of what historical change has revealed about it, namely, that modern democracy is characterized by a radical indeterminacy, a history and politics without guarantees. A radically democratic theory of choice must include a recognition of the inevitability of social antagonism. Such a theory does not strive toward a singular common good defined in the liberal tradition. Rather, choice would involve the possibility of individuals and groups drawing on different traditions. Yet those traditions would be linked to a common political identity defined by radically democratic principles.

At this point we can state a few of the necessary elements or requirements of a school choice plan. (1) Choice needs to be understood as a tool for expanding equitable social relations and for closing down inequitable social relations. Hence, choice always needs to be situated in a broader ethical and political framework. (2) Choice must further a pluralistic ideal to avoid the cultural homogenizing tendencies of the market. (3) Choice being situated in a broader ethical and political framework concerns the limits of pluralism.

In short, I have begun to show the antidemocratic tendencies of market-based choice and suggested some elements necessary for a democratic-based rather than market-based version of school choice. However, the proposal of a democratic form of school choice raises some seemingly intractable problems: How can a theory of school choice mediate between recognition and respect for difference and the need for commonality? And perhaps more critically: Can the language of choice escape the market view that bore it?

First I will discuss the implications of radical democratic theory for school choice and then I will argue the need for moving beyond the language of choice.

Radical democracy's primacy of political principles is highly significant for any democratic form of school choice because if a democratic form of school choice requires a limited pluralism, then radical democratic political principles provide the limits by helping us construct an inside and outside to the political community. Democratic political principles form the nexus around which democratic citizenship and statehood can be imagined. Unlike liberal models that are unable to account for, let alone be constituted by, difference, radical democracy rejects a singular conception of the social good. Instead, radical democracy links multiple different social goods and identities around these democratic principles. Furthermore, those identities and identifications at odds with democratic principles, basic human rights, and social and cultural equality can be excluded. Thus, the framework of democratic political principles forms a framework for a democratic school choice—one that fosters difference and that limits those identifications that are at odds with democracy. Radical democracy allows us to conceive of different individuals and groups struggling for equality to join together to create a new kind of political community. This transformative vision for school choice goes far beyond the status quo versions espoused in the past. Whereas all of the versions of school choice discussed so far accept the political principles of liberal democracy and the liberal subject, a radically democratic theory of choice begins with a reconfiguration of society and the subject.

How does radical democracy reconfigure subjectivity? Radical democracy draws on the deconstructive tradition to recognize that postmodern subjectivity is not a priori but rather unessential and multiply constituted. In short, identity is conceived of not as fixed and static but as the aggregate history of the subject's identifications. Subjects are constructed from the convergence of historical discourses on the body. As such, radical democracy rejects universal or transcendental truths and meanings. Instead, individuals are free to choose those meanings and traditions that contribute to a democratic vision and reject those that do not. While democracy itself is recognized as socially and historically constructed in this view, this does not undermine it. Rather, it strengthens it by revealing that social standards and political principles are not derived from arbitrary inherited rules but are of people's making. Now freed from transcendental truths, people can choose from democratic traditions to make a more ideal society. Furthermore, understanding identity as multiply constituted allows a democratic political theory to comprehend multiple axes of domination and subordination in different contexts. Hence, in this context, choice refers to the possibility of individuals choosing from democratic traditions. Such choices would be limited by those democratic traditions circumscribed by radically democratic political principles.

Radical democracy calls for the creation of a common political identity. However, in accordance with its view of a decentered subject, this common identity is an identity-in-difference. Democratic political principles form a notion of democratic citizenship. This subject position articulates—or links up—with other subject positions. But as Mouffe stresses, radical democratic citizenship is not simply one identity among others. It is *the* common identity. Radical democratic identity thus requires the deconstruction of previous subject positions and the articulation of previous identifications with radical democratic citizenship. This common political identity differs from Habermasian-style interest-group pluralisms, which leave intact group identity and rely for community upon such communicative referents as rationality. Philosopher Nancy Fraser and educational theorist Henry Giroux also offer very clear analyses of the problems with Habermasian attempts at basing a political community on communicative rationality.[22] Both explain the ways that communicative rationality universalizes a particular notion of the common good—namely, a Western, European, androcentric mode of communication. In contrast, Mouffe insists upon a political community defined by no particular singular common good but rather by a set of *political principles* that link multiple goods.

Radical democracy refuses to grant absolute sovereignty to interest groups by rejecting all forms of identity at odds with democratic principles that emerge from the notions of democratic difference, identities, and social relations. Radical democracy includes those identities that foster democratic social relations, such as antiracist, antisexist, anticapitalist, antihomophobic identities, yet excludes those identities that advocate the benefit of one social group at the expense of the greater society. Such antidemocratic identities might include those defined through racism, sexism, homophobia, or capitalism.

A radically democratic theory of school choice thus refuses the individualizing tendencies of liberal democracy and the universalizing tendencies of the liberal subject. As well, it rejects the assumption of a singular common good. It connects the subject and the social to a broader social set of normative political principles. Any theory of school choice would have to be concerned with a recognition of the decentered identities of contemporary individuals and of contemporary democracy. Individuals do not simply choose, or equally choose from an endless array of identifications around them. Identities and identifications are constrained in real material ways by historically forged power relations. For this reason Chantal Mouffe's and Ernesto Laclau's formulation of radical democracy, in which class is yet one more "nodal point" along a chain of identity elements, needs to be tempered with Nancy Fraser's insights about the importance of working toward a radical democracy in which issues of identity and the cultural recognition of subjects are always linked to questions of material distribution. The danger of Laclau's and Mouffe's radical democracy is that it has a tendency to treat economic considerations as yet another identity issue, thereby effacing the importance of a democratic political theory being defined in part through equal economic distribution and distribution of control over the means of production.

Drawing on radical democracy, we can compose a double question: First, a theory of school choice would need to grapple with the political economic question of who controls the means of production and, second, the cultural-linguistic related question of who controls the means of identification production. The answers to these questions are not identical, yet both questions are central to a serious interrogation of the antidemocratic abuse of power and a serious contestation of the erosion of public education. Any meaningfully democratic theory of school choice must grapple with the issues of radically redistributing to the people the control of capital and the control of identification production (meaning-making technologies).

In summation, such a theory of school choice remains committed to Henig's understanding that school choice must be thought of as a tool for the furthering of democracy. However, if school choice needs to be situated in a broader political referent, then radical democracy offers a deeper, more egalitarian model of democracy than liberal democracy. Thinking of school choice in relation to such egalitarian political theories as radical democracy, socialist feminism, and critical pedagogy connects the issue of choice to an understanding of education as a part of a broader democratic social transformation in both the economic and cultural spheres. As well, this radically democratic notion of choice points to the special role of teachers as cultural workers engaged in producing radically democratic identifications and student identities.

Beyond the Language of Choice and toward the Language of Democracy

Despite its potential as an equity-expanding tool, the principal danger of the choice metaphor in the contemporary context is that it redefines public social relationships in private ways. First, vouchers and tax credits redirect money and students in a way that transforms collective decisions into private decisions. The dangers of this are most apparent in the case of market-based choice, in which local community control over schools is often given over to corporations based elsewhere. The bottom line and the interests of the corporate board then determine the decisions affecting the school. Communal control is lost.

In the case of liberal voucher plans the privatizing of public decision making is less obvious but still dangerous. While liberal voucher plans do not envision transforming the schools into profit-making entities for the wealthy the way market-based choice does, the introduction of vouchers into public education undermines a strong sense of the possibility of broad-based authoritative government action to reverse current inequalities by shifting deliberation, decision-making, agency, and direct delivery out of the hands of the government and into private hands. Public schools are more than the places where children learn. They are a public forum and the locus of democratic decision making. Faith in the public sphere and in public institutions is at an all-time low. The privatizing of educational decision making further undermines and weakens the public sphere by suggesting a public ineffectual and incapable of steering social forces. This logic furthers the dangerous parallel logic that mistakenly views the economy as autonomous and places human well-being in Adam Smith's invisible fist.

The metaphor of choice in the contemporary context also idealizes business. Hence, democratic decisions framed in market terms of consumption tend to conflate democratic participation with shopping. Education is a public good, not a private service. The metaphor of choice, which is currently being used to justify the privatization of public utilities, undermines the idea that the public owns public entities. Rather, public entities are represented by this term as a private consumer commodity.

Perhaps one of the most dangerous aspects of vouchers is that they profoundly redefine education from being a social good to being an entitlement.

The significance of this shift should not be understated. Those public entities thought to be social goods, such as national defense, public roads, and policing, are considered universally necessary and unquestionable elements of a democracy. Entitlements, on the other hand, are less secure in that they are viewed as being in the special interest of a group rather than of the entire society. Vouchers are generally thought of as entitlements. Welfare, Medicare, Medicaid, social security, and other social services are thought of as entitlements.

> Today, the concept of providing an in-kind government subsidy in a voucherlike form is a familiar one. The best-known example is the federal food stamp program. Begun in the early 1960s, the program quickly grew; each month it now provides over twenty million lower-income Americans with coupons that can be used to purchase groceries. Section 8, a housing program, represents another important voucher program. Initiated in 1974, Section 8 provides certificates to some lower-income families to supplement their ability to afford to rent in the private housing market. Programs like Medicaid and Medicare, which provide government reimbursement to medical providers who treat, respectively, the eligible poor and the elderly, are not literally voucher programs, in that they do not provide a redeemable chit to the beneficiary. But they are philosophical kin in most important respects. Like vouchers, they provide in-kind benefits rather than cash, and like vouchers they are intended to enable beneficiaries to meet their needs in the private sector.[23]

This was written in 1994. Two years later the widespread dismantling of voucher-based welfare entitlements passed federal and state legislatures. In short, the reassignment of public education as an entitlement via the use of vouchers risks redefining public school as an entitlement from which public support can be withdrawn. In light of the mounting threats to the public sphere, the broader privatization movement, and the redefining of the corporate good as the public good, the use of vouchers even for equitable aims risks undermining the democratic tradition of public education as universal social good. More important, this risks losing public schools as a site of struggle for the radical democratization of all social spheres.

NOTES

   1. Maria Newman, "10 Districts Are Named in Test of School Choice," *New York Times,* 1 December 1999, 8B.
   2. Presently, the top 5 percent of the economy controls 79 percent of the wealth. The real wage has been declining steadily since 1973. Since 1970 the number of

people working multiple jobs increased by 44 percent. (Popular Economics Workshop of the Western Pennsylvania Living Wage Campaign [A Project of the Alliance for Progressive Action]). The richest 1 percent of American families have nearly as much wealth as the bottom 95 percent; between 1980 and 1993, salaries for American CEOs increased by 514 percent while workers' wages rose by 68 percent, well behind inflation. See Holly Sklar, *Chaos or Community? Seeking Solutions, Not Scapegoats for Bad Economics* (Boston: South End, 1995), 5–10, 55–56.

3. See Jonathan Kozol, *Savage Inequalities* (New York: Crown, 1991).

4. Adam Smith proposed educational vouchers in the eighteenth century.

5. See Stanley Aronowitz and William DiFazio, *The Jobless Future* (Minneapolis: University of Minnesota Press, 1994). See also Upton Sinclair's *The Jungle* for a chilling account of an America before sufficient government regulation on consumables. It is important to note that it was the hard work of unions that got much consumer protection passed.

6. See Charles Derber, *Corporation Nation* (New York: St. Martin's, 1998), 212.

7. While the economic basis for slavery is more obvious, both segregation and disenfranchisement derive from power struggles that in the last instance are material.

8. Newman, "10 Districts Are Named in Test of School Choice," B8.

9. Jeffrey Henig, *Rethinking School Choice* (Princeton, N.J.: Princeton University Press, 1994), 191–192.

10. John E. Coons and Stephen D. Sugarman, *Education by Choice: The Case for Family Control* (Berkeley: University of California Press, 1978).

11. Henig, *Rethinking School Choice,* 24.

12. See Henry A. Giroux, *Border Crossings: Cultural Workers and the Politics of Education* (New York: Routledge, 1992), in particular the chapter entitled "Modernism, Postmodernism, and Feminism," for an explication of the need to draw on various theoretical traditions to rethink actually existing democracy in order to form a more egalitarian and pluralistic democratic ideal toward which educators and other cultural workers can struggle. See Chantal Mouffe, *The Return of the Political* (New York: Verso, 1992), for a formulation of radical democracy as distinct from liberal democratic theories such as Rawls's.

13. Charles Taylor, *Multiculturalism and the Politics of Recognition* (Princeton: Princeton University Press, 1992), 25.

14. The invention of race or the racializing of social subjects and racist discourse are, of course, not merely functional tools to justify economic pursuits. The racializing of social subjects, as David Theo Goldberg explains, is a central feature of modernism and needs to be understood as built into modernist discourses such as liberalism. For a history of the invention of race at the locus of modernist discourse and material realities, see David Theo Goldberg, *Racist Culture* (Cambridge: Blackwell, 1993).

15. Robin D. G. Kelley, *Yo Mama's Dysfunktional!* (Boston: Beacon, 1997), 7.

16. See Herman Gray, *Watching Race: Television and the Struggle for Blackness* (Minneapolis: University of Minnesota Press, 1995).

17. See Judith Arren and Christopher Jencks, "Education Vouchers: A Proposal for Diversity and Choice," in George R. La Noue, *Educational Vouchers, Concepts and Controversies* (New York: Teachers College Press, 1972), 53. See also Theodore R. Sizer, "The Case for a Free Market," originally published in *Saturday Review* (11 January 1969); reprinted in *Education Vouchers: From Theory to Alum Rock,* ed. James A. Mecklenburger and Richard W. Hostrop (Homewood, Ill.: ETC Publications, 1972), 30.

18. Testimony before the Committee on Education and Labor, April 2, 1971.

19. Henig, *Rethinking School Choice,* 17.

20. Mouffe, *The Return of the Political,* 4.

21. Mouffe, *The Return of the Political,* 3–4.

22. See Nancy Fraser, *Unruly Practices* (Minneapolis: University of Minnesota Press, 1989), and *Justice Interruptus* (New York: Routledge, 1997) and Henry Giroux, *Border Crossings* (New York: Routledge, 1992).

23. Henig, *Rethinking School Choice,* 63.

3

Coca-Cola and the Commercialization of Public Schools

In March of 1998 a sensational story splashed onto the pages of newspapers nationwide.[1] Gloria Hamilton, principal of Greenbrier High School in Evans, Georgia, suspended a student for wearing a Pepsi T-shirt on "Coke Day." "Coke in Education Day" was the high school's entry into the "Team Up with Coca-Cola" contest. The contest encourages students to devise plans to distribute promotional Coke discount cards locally. Greenbrier's "Coke in Education Day" entry involved a day of Coke rallies, speeches by Coke executives, economics classes about Coke's marketing tactics, chemistry classes analyzing the sugar content in Coke, and the culminating activity—an aerial photograph of the students' bodies dressed in red and white and forming the word *Coke*. Seniors were the letter "C," juniors "o," sophomores "k," and freshmen "e." The reward for winning the district-wide contest—$500. Winning locally also qualified the school to enter a national contest to sell Coke products for $10,000.

During the photo shoot, two students removed their outer shirts to reveal Pepsi shirts. The students were sent to the principal's office and given one-day in-school suspensions. Principal Hamilton justified her decision to punish the students, insisting that the incident was strictly a matter of student behavior.

"It's not a Coke–Pepsi war issue. It has nothing to do with that. It was a student deliberately being disruptive and rude." She also said that the punishment was for "trying to destroy the school picture."[2] The principal's statement about the "school picture" refers to the corporate contest photograph. In another statement the principal admitted that the suspensions were, in fact, very much tied to the visit by the large corporation that is headquartered just a short distance away.

It really would have been acceptable if it had just been in-house, but we had
the regional president here and people flew in from Atlanta to do us the honor
of being resource speakers. These students knew we had guests.[3]

The student who received the most attention for the act, Mike Cameron, told
reporters, "I don't consider this a prank. I like to be an individual. That's the
way I am."

In the press frenzy that followed the event, a media consensus emerged that
viewed the principal's actions as unjust, extreme, and an incursion into individual liberty and freedom of speech. Most of the papers framed the event
humorously and many interpreted it as a marketing and business event, placing the article in the business section. However, only a few publications carried articles pointing to the issue of the commercialization of the public
schools. These more critical articles largely appeared at least a week after the
incident. The majority of the press respondents concluded that the principal
had been excessive in her disciplinary response. The principal's discipline
seemed excessive to most writers largely on the grounds that she was squelch-
ing a student's freedom of choice. Choice in this context is defined economically. Individual freedom becomes an issue here when the choice being constrained is consumer choice. When students are subject to searches, urine
testing, surveillance, or other losses of individual freedom, it seldom makes
the news.[4] Several articles, even those critical of the principal's actions, suggested that corporate profiteering in schools is not a problem. Rather, they
suggested that this is a legitimate source of funding. Few articles discussed
the matter in terms of the growing commercialization of the public schools
and the threat it poses to education as a public good. For example, the *Wall
Street Journal* framed the event as an episode in the "cola wars." It may make
more sense, however, to understand the incident in terms of class war and
culture war.

THE COMMERCIALIZATION OF PUBLIC SCHOOLS

The rise of commercialization in public schools has been extensively studied.[5]
Efforts to turn public school students into a captive market have succeeded
with the continuation of KIII's Channel One, corporate-written curricula, partnerships, contests, exclusive contracts on vending, as well as the transformation of school hallways, school buses, book covers, and scoreboards into corporate advertisements. In Denver, Colorado, Coke wrote a letter to principals
instructing them to allow students virtually unlimited access to Coke machines
and to move the machines to where they would be "accessible to the students

all day." John Bushey, the official who manages the contract, wrote, "Research shows that vendor purchases are closely linked to availability," adding, "location, location, location is the key."[6] "The soft drink companies are turning schools into virtual sales agents for their products," says Andrew Hagelshaw, senior program director of the Center for Commercial-Free Public Education, a nonprofit group based in Oakland, California. "These kinds of contracts are going to change the priorities from education to soda consumption."[7]

Consider these other examples:

Denver, Houston, Newark, and Jefferson County, Colorado[,]school districts have set up soft-drink or marketing programs.[8]

Pepsi gave 1.5 million for a new sports stadium and county schools tested a new science course, developed in part by Pepsi, titled "The Carbonated Beverage Company," in which students taste-test colas, analyze cola samples, take a video tour of a Pepsi bottling plant and visit a local Pepsi plant.[9]

Commercialization initiatives in public schools can be broken down into two types: (1) so-called educative and (2) straight promotional. The first kind cloaks itself as educative. Channel One presents itself as a news program for teaching current events but really exists to sell commercial time to sponsors hawking pizza, soft drinks, clothing, and other consumer goods. Even if the news content of Channel One (which has been characterized as laughable, antiquated, uncritical, and shallow) offered substance for intellectual debate, the commercials would not need to be there for educational use. Similarly,

A new company called ZapMe! is offering schools thousands of dollars worth of computer equipment, including a satellite dish, fifteen state of the art personal computers, a furnished computer lab and high-speed Internet access—all for free. The catch: The computers display a constant stream of on-screen advertisements in the lower left-hand corner of the screen.[10]

Companies such as Lifetime Learning send curriculum plans to teachers for free. These prefab curricula take advantage of teachers who are hard-pressed by bureaucratic constraints and heavy workloads. Ultimately, the curricula take advantage of children by depriving them of meaningful education and by not only often promoting unhealthy products and misinformation but by also pushing crass consumerism.

Eager to attract young customers, companies such as General Mills and Campbell Soup provide free classroom materials that blatantly hawk their products. For instance, "General Mills has sent 8,000 teachers a science curriculum on volcanoes entitled 'Gushers: Wonders of the Earth,' which uses the

company's fruit gushers candy." Similarly, *The Washington Post* reported recently
that McDonald's provides free curriculum packages to elementary schools in
which students learn about how McDonald's restaurant is run and, in case they
miss the point about future job opportunities, they also learn how to apply for
employment at the fast food chain.[11]

Often, as a 1995 Consumers Union study found, the "information kits" contain incomplete information, procorporate propaganda, and outright lies.

According to "Captive Kids: A Report on Commercial Pressures on Kids at
School," published in 1995 by Consumer Reports, nearly 80 percent of the 100
SEMs (sponsored educational materials) examined contained "biased or incomplete information" in a way that "favors the company or its agenda." An exercise book purports to teach junior high math by having kids plan an "end-term
Domino's pizza party." (Question: "How much pizza should we buy?" Answer:
"It was determined that we would eat 74 slices from a 16″ pizza. [Therefore]
we should order nine 16″ and one 12″ pizzas from our local Domino's pizza
store.")[12]

A science kit distributed by the Campbell Soup Company, which makes Prego
spaghetti sauce, contained an experiment in which kids use "scientific thinking"
to prove that Prego is thicker than Ragu.

Procter & Gamble, the nation's largest manufacturer of disposable diapers,
once distributed learning materials called "Decision: Earth," which taught kids
that disposable diapers are better for the environment than the cloth variety.

Nutrition lessons sponsored by Kellogg's presented fat content as the sole concern when choosing a breakfast food. The sugar & sodium levels of cereals were
not mentioned.

Learning materials distributed by the National Coal Foundation failed to
mention any of the problems with coal and actually dismissed the greenhouse
effect. "The earth could benefit rather than be harmed from increased carbon
dioxide . . . ," it said.[13]

In addition to advertising masquerading as curriculum, commercialization
in public schools takes the form of direct corporate promotion often presented
as corporate community service. This more direct form of profiteering in
schools often goes by the name of "partnerships." These partnerships have
become increasingly legitimized in the wake of the *A Nation at Risk* report
and allow corporations such as Citibank, McDonald's, IBM, or Coca-Cola to
appear to support public education while actually engaging in marketing
goods, services, or corporate image to youth. The incursion of corporations
into public schooling is usually justified by the funds brought to public education. However, as Alex Molnar explains, the actual amount of money that

corporations give public schools is minuscule relative to the needs created by corporate-led government cutbacks in social spending.

In 1989, total corporate contributions to public elementary schools totaled $156 million. Corporate contributions to private schools and to colleges and universities totaled $2.4 billion in the same year. Considered from another angle, $156 million is a tiny fraction of the $1 billion plus in tax breaks that Wisconsin corporations alone received each year from the state of Wisconsin in the late 1990s. By one estimate, total corporate contributions to kindergarten through twelfth-grade (K–12) education in 1990 would run the nation's schools for less than two hours.[14]

The corporate tax drain caused by successful corporate lobbying against taxes and social spending has contributed to public schools—particularly urban and nonwhite public schools—being incapable of raising sufficient funds. The result of the depleted tax base has been the defunding of those areas already hardest hit by corporate firings and the flight of business from the urban center and from the nation. The most injured parties of the corporate pursuit of profit are the first to be targeted for profiteering in the form of "partnerships" and other privatization initiatives. In short, then, the issue of corporate involvement in public schooling cannot be considered separately from the history of the corporate evasion of social responsibility. Corporations, which represent the upper strata of wealthy citizens, have been paying consistently fewer taxes since the 1930s. Corporations have successfully lobbied the government for the freedom to export American jobs abroad. Treaties such as GATT and NAFTA were corporate-led and have benefited a corporate elite domestically and abroad. The steady upward redistribution of wealth since the Reagan era, the decrease in the quality of work, the steady decrease in the real wage, and the elimination of worker benefits are all a part of the triumph of corporate culture. The decrease in workers' real wages during economic booms such as in the late '90s suggests the overwhelming power of corporate culture to define the national agenda and to facilitate the upward redistribution of wealth.[15]

In terms of the Coke case, the corporate economic agenda is clear. The Coca-Cola company, which has participated in defunding public schooling, can appear to support public schooling by offering prize money to schools that create the best Coke advertising. Interestingly, the schools are forced to compete against each other for the money. Of course, if Coca-Cola were genuinely interested in helping to fund American public education, it would not force schools to compete for the money or force them to sell Coke. However, even if Coke were to give public schools grants, this would reinforce a highly private way of thinking of education that is founded in volunteerism and philanthropy rather than in a recognition of the need for public support for public goods. Volunteerism and philanthropy cannot be relied on to fund properly universal quality education. For this reason, the necessary corporate funding of education must come from public taxes on corporations.[16]

Corporations are the single biggest recipient of public funding. Many studies reveal that the dominant justifications for corporate welfare are unfounded.[17] Corporate welfare is often justified on the grounds that corporations create jobs and stimulate the economy. However, nationally, corporate welfare does not result in the creation of more jobs.[18] New jobs are usually exported to other countries where cheap labor is exploited. The public often funds companies that then drain jobs from the economy. Studies have conclusively shown that corporate welfare does not create jobs. As well, corporate welfare does not benefit the economy because commerce is global in character, and capital is becoming increasingly more mobile. Not only are jobs exported overseas, but profits are often reinvested in foreign investments. Public subsidies for private profiteers cannot be justified as anything other than an upward redistribution of wealth. Estimates on the extent of corporate welfare range from around $150 billion a year to $450 billion.[19] Not only should this money be used to fund social services that benefit the bulk of the population and those in need, but, in addition, corporations, our wealthiest citizens, need to shoulder a fair burden of the cost of public education.

Some newspaper writers on the Coke suspension case did make the connection between the defunding of the public schools and the behavior of corporations. Sara Eckel writes,

> As shameless and vulgar as the above examples are, we cannot blame corporate America if they get into our kids' classrooms. Companies exist to make money, and they will go after that money any way they can even if it means exploiting schoolkids. It is our job as taxpayers and as citizens to keep them from crossing that line. And the best way to do that is to ensure that public schools get the funding they need so that they can say no to these deals with the devil.[20]

Eckel points to the way the logic of capital, the logic of the bottom line, contains no ethical or political constraint. If any benefits accrue to the public as the result of the actions of corporations, they are largely incidental to the private pursuit of profit. Eckel's point about the need for a strong public to constrain the actions of corporations is well taken. However, perhaps the issue runs a bit deeper to the question of whether corporations ought to be allowed to exist at all in their present state.

Historically, in colonial times until the nineteenth century, as Richard Grossman has shown, corporations only came into being as the result of publicly ordained charters. These charters allowed a corporation to perform an act such as building a road. When the task of the corporation was completed, the corporation would legally dissolve. The public could at any time revoke a corporation's charter when the actions of the corporation appeared to run counter to the public interest. As well, the dissolution of corporations meant that corporations could not be perpetual profit machines, nor could they speculate, thereby profiting from unproductive behavior. By allowing corporations to exist as individuals, the law gives up public control over corporate actions. As a result, the corporation is not constrained by the public good. In a democracy, corporations should be constrained by the public in order to prevent the interests of an economic elite from benefiting at the expense of the bulk of the population.

Allison Berryhill also discusses the relationship between the defunding of public schools and the actions of corporations. She writes,

> Our willingness to sell out our schools grows in direct proportion to our unwillingness to amply fund education. Budget-strapped schools hunger for the tidbits corporations dangle in exchange for access to students. And $10,000 toward field trips and textbooks starts to look like pretty good pay for lining kids up to spell out "Coke" in front of the corporate cameras. If we do not amply fund our schools, advertisers' dollars will remain tantalizing—though not easy to digest. Mark Twain said it well: "I was obliged to eat [the apples], I was so hungry. It was against my principles, but I find that principles have no real force except when one is well fed."[21]

Berryhill's remarks raise the issue of the way the defunding of public schools creates a desperation for funding. Such desperation leads to the portrayal of corporate profiteers as saviors rather than parasites. Of course, the corporate behavior that leads to the defunding in the first place is not commonly spoken of in mass media or in educational policy circles. A preponderance of mass media representations of corporations as "responsible citizens" works in conjunction with corporate volunteerism deceptively to portray corporations as concerned with the public good.

Berryhill's comments point to another issue as well. Namely, the economic struggles over public school funding are intertwined with cultural struggles over public meaning. Economic shifts have not been the only changes wrought by the right-wing revolution. Corporations have successfully redefined culture. In an era of the gutting of the public sphere, public schools are one of the few forums left for public deliberation and decision making. The corporate threat to public schools is a threat not only to a democratic form of education but to democracy itself.

Since the onset of the culture of Reaganism, academics, policymakers, and cultural workers in mass media have increasingly justified American education on the macroeconomic grounds of economic efficiency. Schooling should produce workers who can compete for America in the global economy. Education has also been increasingly justified as a source of upward social mobility for individuals. These economic bases for education stand at odds with a broader democratic vision. Education becomes thought of as a means to assimilate students into an economy not of their making. In part, democratic control of the economy would mean that the bulk of the population is involved in decisions about what kinds of work they do, what kinds of working conditions, benefits, and security they receive. Education for economic efficiency aims to reproduce rather than transform existing conditions. It keeps an economic and cultural elite in control of decisions that affect most citizens. Education for democracy, on the contrary, contests the concentration of deliberative power, economic power, and cultural-valuational power. As well, the upward mobility justification for education hinders its democratic potential. Upward mobility makes the promise of education an individual rather than a social promise. It redefines education as an individual good rather than a public good. This makes education into a consumer choice, further opening the door to antidemocratic privatization initiatives.

CORPORATE CULTURE

In what follows I will discuss the way the corporatization of public schools works on multiple symbolic levels. Before I do, I want to stress that the economic and cultural struggles that play out in schools cannot be seen independently. For example, Coke's successful redefinition of students as consumers is both an economic and a cultural project. The Coke corporation has a specific financial interest in such identity formation, yet such a cultural transformation cannot be understood as a merely economic effect. As I will discuss, part of Coke's cultural pedagogy involves an attempt to enact a quasi-religious ritualization of its product. The medieval vision underlying Coke's cultural pedagogy is fundamentally a political project that positions the corporation as a benevolent lord and positions citizens as peasants dependent upon the benevolence of the corporation.

While this antidemocratic political vision does emerge from economic pursuits, it creates a cultural and political climate that forms the conditions for the transformation of social relations. In keeping with the same example, the redefinition of students as consumers and possible future employees transforms the social view of the meaning of public education. When the public good becomes subordinated to the corporate good, it becomes possible to enact policies that further this on an economic level. Hence, a school day becomes dedicated to selling Coke product. In part, it is important to remember the partial autonomy of the cultural and economic spheres because resistance to capitalist exploitation and transformation of the social in a more democratic fashion requires a strong sense of the public good. As well, these social relations that are structured in domination can be transformed with struggle and resistance. The fostering of a strong sense of the public good is not only an economic project but also a more overarching social one—economic, cultural, and political.

Coke's cultural pedagogy works on the content of the curriculum. It also works on bodies—students', teachers', and administrators' bodies by shaping desires, needs, and how resources and space are constructed. It works on the broader public discourse surrounding education. It defines how education is justified. Corporatization also does a stealthy job of erasing the reality of certain social relations and producing new fictitious narratives in their stead. For example, in the Coke Day scandal the reality of the production process of Coca-Cola was erased and replaced with a deceptive facsimile of this process, followed by an enactment of the image of the product. Students took economics classes about Coke marketing and studied the sugar content in Coke in chemistry class. Such simulations of lessons of the product's history avoid broader economic, political, and power-sensitive questions such as what class, race, and gender of people drive Coke trucks and what class, race, and gender sit on the board of directors? Do bottling-plant workers get decent pay, benefits, and job security? How big is the income differential of the highest-paid and lowest-paid Coke worker? Does the dumping and heavy marketing of a product with no nutritional value in poor countries struggling for nutritional food suggest Coca-Cola is involved in international exploitation? Are foreign workers paid on par with domestic ones? Nor did the Coke Day lessons approach questions pertaining to the social value of the product. Should children anywhere be sold food products with negative nutritional value—tooth-destroying, diabetes-inducing, attention-span-shortening sugar and caffeine that cause hyperactivity? In light of the epidemic proportions of attention deficit disorder (ADD) and attention deficit hyperactivity disorder (ADHD) diagnoses in American public schools, should parents and teachers consider that children are being medically treated for symptoms caused by heavily marketed, omnipresent, processed, health-destroying "foods" such as

Coca-Cola? Are medical industries such as the pharmaceutical giants getting rich off the problems caused by the food and beverage industry? One thing is certain. In Coke's marketing and in the Coke Day exercises the history, power relations, and politics of the corporation and the product remain absent from the public image that the product assumes.

Bodies

What can we read in the bodies of students lined up in a schoolyard to spell out the name of a mass-marketed product? On one level we can read a transformation—students objectified in the most real and tangible sense. Students' bodies are transformed into living, breathing advertisements for a corporate product. The loss of the self, the loss of individuality, the renunciation of difference within the united colors of Coke. Can we read something in the fact that the students' bodies composed not a picture of the product, not a can of Coke but the word *Coke?*

Critical educators such as Paulo Freire, Henry Giroux, and bell hooks have shown the relationships between language, power, possibility, and social transformation. Freire stresses the critical reading of the word to read the world to transform the world. Giroux insists that education must be meaningful to become critical to become transformative. Similarly, hooks suggests the need for critical literacy in order to foster social transformation. Common to all three theorists is a recognition that one role of radical educators is to teach critical reading as a means to help students theorize their experience, to develop an ability to critically understand the world, and ultimately to transform the world in a more just and equal and less oppressive fashion. This being the case, what happens when the student becomes the word? Is the Coca-Cola company successfully collapsing individual subjectivity into language, such that language itself disappears into the bodies of youth and bodies renounce themselves as mere signifiers in the service of consumerism?

Such a claim would perhaps overstate the power of the Coca-Cola corporation's schoolyard exercise. However, when the Coke company coerces students to enact the product through language, it promotes a very overt corporate justification for language. Language for corporations exists in the service of profiteering by an elite, not in the service of human freedom, emancipation, or democracy. Language in corporate culture connects to the corporate justification for schooling itself—namely, schooling to produce consumers who will buy Coke and keep the corporate machine rolling. Language produces corporate identities as well as precluding students from imagining noncorporate identity. For example, Mike Cameron resists corporate exploitation by Coke by embracing corporate exploitation by Pepsi. Individuality is defined in terms of individual consumption rather than in democratic ways concerned with the relationship of the individual to the public good and social responsibility. The Coca-Cola corporation need not be concerned with strong public schools to produce the managers it will need to run the company and market the product globally. It can always get these students from private schools attended by the most privileged segment of the population. Democratic schooling concerned with the maintenance of a strong public sphere does not serve corporate interests. The Coca-Cola company is not concerned with the dangers to democracy posed by the social and cultural reproduction of an economic elite. Coca-Cola is a part of this elite.

Perhaps we can on another level understand Coke's collapse of bodies and language as a metaphor for what Coke is doing to students. As students' bodies become signifiers for a mass-marketed commodity, both language and student bodies are subordinated to the image of the commodity. What we witness in the schoolyard could be thought of as a symbolic ritual, almost a religious ritual in which students are compelled to abandon their individual sovereignty to the symbolic realm. Individuality disappears into the massified symbol of the object. "Coke Day" could be understood as a new religious holiday, a ritual that actively reconstitutes the faith in the commodity to provide for us. Indeed, the school principal's outrage at Mike Cameron stemmed from his irreverence toward those bishops in the Coke-Church hierarchy—the corporate executives. Cameron's donning of the vestments of heresy—the Pepsi T-shirt—begat excommunication. Translating the event into religious terms risks creating an absurdist extended metaphor. However, this metaphor aptly illustrates the antidemocratic, irrational, and faith-bound nature of commodity worship and the faith in the market—faith in a deity that doesn't come through for most worshipers.

Becoming the word speaks to Judeo-Christian religious traditions. In Judaism the dead live on in the prayers of the living. On Yom Kippur, one becomes inscribed in God's book of life. More pertinently, Christianity suggests that God on earth, Jesus, is the word made flesh. These student bodies spell out the sacred symbol of the absent, benevolent, and almighty Coke/God. The word made flesh, student bodies stand for the elevated and absent product, Coke, whose mysteries of production are replaced by the earthly symbol, the stylized word. The commodity image replaces the effaced production process. The image of Coke replaces and eclipses the social relations involved in the manufacture, distribution, and marketing of the product. Consuming Coke becomes divorced from the history of production. The imagery replaces this history with certain emotional and visceral associations. The current slogan for Coca-Cola speaks to this process: "Always Coca-Cola." Timeless and infinite, beyond human control, beyond even the control of nature, Coke is not made by people but is an unmoved mover, a creator with its own creation unaccounted for.

Just as Christ stands in for or replaces God by embodying the absent and invisible deity, the students stand in for or replace the absent product. Christ as replacement for God is simultaneously God in the form of Christ. Coke, a product that is usually taken in, ingested by humans, exteriorizes into an abstract symbolic form, the word, and takes in or ingests human beings. In a straightforward symbolic way the reversal of the product and the human suggests the Coke corporation's social vision. Namely, people subject to the product; people consumed by the product; people in the service of and sacrificed for the product.

Walter Benjamin wrote of the fundamental change in representations that occurs with the rise of the reproducible image. The aura of authenticity emanates from the original image/ object. Benjamin locates a shift in the function of art with the rise of the reproducible image and the disappearance of the original. The ritual function of art that was tied to the authenticity of the original object falls, only to be replaced by the political function of art. For Benjamin, this shift accompanies a fundamental change in human temporal-spatial relations to the object. With the rise of the reproducible image, the physical distance between the subject and the object begins to collapse. A painting is contemplated from a distance. One holds off the image and takes it in. Successively, with the photograph and then the motion picture, the increased speed of apprehension of the image renders the human decreasingly capable of holding off the image. Rather, the human begins to be taken in by the image/object. The rapid-fire sequence of the film frames, for example, prohibits critical contemplation of each individual frame. The loss of critical distance renders an individual unable to hold off the image. According to Benjamin, the loss of an object's history, the loss of the object's authenticity creates in people an urge to get closer to the object to reach the missing aura of originality. What is grasped is only the reproduction. "Every day the urge grows stronger to get hold of an object at very close range by way of its likeness, its reproduction."[22]

Whereas Benjamin, in this essay, discusses art objects rather than consumable commodities, the consumable commodity since Benjamin's time has taken on the character of the reproducible image. Coca-Cola is a black, bubbly substance with a distinctive flavor. Yet what is sold is not this turgid oil-looking goo but the image of Coca-Cola, associations with the product. The red and white can, the red and white logo, the distinctive lettering, the jingle, the slogan, are all reproduced. There is no original. Yet Coke claims originality right on the can and the bottle. Ritualization occurs in Coke advertising. Winter marketing associates Coke with Christmas symbols, while summer advertising associates Coke with the oldest god, the sun. Coke appeals to originality in its appeal to tradition right on the can. Coca-Cola refers to itself on the can as "classic."

As a mass-produced image endlessly reproduced over TV and movie screens, Coke falsely promises the missing aura of authenticity. Coke is the "real thing." "Coke is it." Perhaps we can read in the Coke Day rituals the ultimate result of the collapse of subject–object relations with the loss of critical distance that comes with the accelerated apprehension of the reproduced image. "Every day the urge grows stronger to get hold of an object at very close range by way of its likeness, its reproduction."[23] In the Coke Day ritual students attempt to get hold of the elusive object by becoming it. Their bodies become the Coke symbol, which is in fact the essence of Coca-Cola— namely, its image.

I have located in the Coke Day event a certain reversal of subject and object. Students are transformed by the company into the product. Could this be the ultimate marketing tactic? Typically, consumers are taught to identify with a popularly positive association with the product. What more effective form of identification could there be than identification as the product itself? To consume Coke in this instance becomes redefined not as an act of consuming oneself, or of consuming life, or of consuming the mass of one's fellow students. Rather, as the individual becomes the product, s/he becomes the object of consumption desired by all the world. One takes on the esteem and prestige of this holy object—an object so sacred and symbolic of social value in some developing countries as to be placed on the mantel, the showpiece of the whole dwelling.

However, outside of Atlanta, as students become the object of consumer desire, they project themselves into the commodity and desire themselves there. They want to be consumed, worshiped, and revered as the sacred object. Is this the culmination and limit of consumerism when individuals do not merely desire commodities but desire to be desired as commodities? We don't just *want* these sacred things. We want *to be* them. We want to be desired as they are desired, consumed as they are consumed, coveted, sought after, prized, elevated, and endlessly reproduced such that we approach the interminable infinity of the almighty (God/commodity). This is the central problem of consumer culture. It produces desire in the service of assimilation, homogeneity, the abandonment of individual uniqueness; it tends toward massification, undifferentiation, brutal acriticality, and docility. The formation of consumer identities, which comes from the pedagogies of consumer culture, is not merely a matter of making individuals who define themselves by what they can possess and consume. It is also a matter of making individuals who no longer possess the critical capacity to envision a different, better future.

The corporate destruction of the capacity to imagine a better future is about competing understandings of time. "Always Coca-Cola"—Coca-Cola has always been here and always will be here. In the corporate flattening of time to an infinite presentism, imagining a better future becomes impossible. The only option becomes losing oneself in the promise of the eternalized present— a present in which one can only obey the advertising command, "Enjoy Coke." This is also about a struggle over distance. As Benjamin realized, the collapse of the subject into the object involves a loss of critical distance. As the individual becomes the object, becomes the image, there can be no criticality, contestation, holding off and contemplating the object.

Is this the ultimate form of objectification? Is there a way to intercede in this process or a way to push this objectification in such a way as to commit a kind of aikido move, swinging the aggressive power of consumerism against itself? Contestation or transformation? By discussing the power of the image à la Benjamin's ideas, I risk giving the impression that agency stems not from corporations and their leaders but from images and objects. On the contrary, I would now like to discuss the ways that capitalist modes of representation are not natural but rather are painstakingly constituted and actively disseminated by specific individuals and to insist that individuals must take responsibility for the pedagogies and social visions contained in their cultural products.

A great deal of writing in contemporary philosophy and cultural studies locates the origins of social problems strictly within the history of a transcendentalizing logic that has characterized Western metaphysics since Plato. This anti-utopian argument, which comes out of Nietzsche,[24] suggests that the quasi-religious transcendentality of metaphysics issues a logic of deferral, idealism, and nonpresence such that attempts at fixing truth and being are fundamentally fictions, due to the changing nature of the world and the slippage of meaning inherent in language. While someone such as Derrida is concerned precisely with the question of the simultaneous impossibility and necessity of metaphysical thinking, the strict focus, particularly among textually based academics, on Western traditions of thought elides structural and material historical conditions for present social relations structured in domination. Such an approach fails to give adequate due to power struggles or even the development of new technologies that also guide shifts in thought.

If, as many textual-based theorists argue, there is an inevitable slippage be-tween language and meaning, between language and being, an inevitable trans-cendentality at the base of thought, a looking elsewhere, then there would seem to be competition for what the subject looks to. When Nietzsche saw the death of God, he saw a crisis of vision for the next two hundred years. If Westerners do not look to God to ground experience, truth, and meaning, then where do they look? The self, Nature, science and technology, a whole series of transcendental ideals that presume progress, a Judeo-Christian messianism or eschatology. The utopian projects of the '60s such as liberation theology are no less founded in this quasi-religious eschatology.

However, as Benjamin Barber has suggested, the present is seeing a glo-bal struggle between corporate and fundamentalist visions of progress. While corporate visions adhere to a blind faith in progress and technology without accepting the historical failures of technology to bring up the bulk of the world's population, fundamentalism puts all its eggs in the basket of spiri-tual ecstasy and the promise of the afterlife. In short, the philosophical focus on the problem of a kind of thinking—deferred thinking (representational thought, transcendentality, metaphysics of nonpresence, utopian thought)—like the obsessions with "textual politics" or the "endless play of significa-tion," currently so common in the business of academia, refuses to engage politically in the ways future visions and promises are constructed by pow-erful interests and have real material effects. The focus on the form that thought takes (this can be found in Deleuze's celebration of rhizomatics) also fails to recognize that forms of thought do not guarantee liberating power relations. As well, blaming utopian thought for social problems refuses to admit that practice contains theoretical content, and hence practice inevita-bly implies future visions. Whether recognized or not, all practice for good or bad contains future vision or what might be called a utopian or transcen-dent dimension. Whether recognized or not, practices compete for the future. Educators and cultural workers need their practices to emerge from a demo-cratic, egalitarian vision rather than one founded in greed, exploitation, self-ish indifference to others, or an abandonment of criticality and agency.

The practice of critical education competes against Coke's papal antidemo-cratic vision. Critical educators such as Giroux insist upon a utopian philoso-phy of hope as a first principle of meaningful theoretical work. The language of critique must be followed by a language of possibility to move beyond institutionally commodified academic debate and the comfortable reward of cynical righteousness. Critical educational theory should articulate with emancipatory social struggle to "provide potentially liberating forms of cri-tique and the theoretical basis for new forms of social relations."[25]

Coke's vision, which offers individuals the markets' consumption-utopia (Coke also makes Fruitopia), stands at odds with the critical pedagogical vision of transformation toward a genuine democracy. Yet Coke has all the power of marketing science and psychological research and the power of institutions behind it. How can a critical vision compete against the ecstatic promise of market pedagogy that allows individuals the television-style easy abdication of the self to the commodity/image?

One possibility lends itself to the project of intervening in the collapse of subject–object relations that comes with consumer pedagogies. This possibility is a strategy of intervention to maintain a critical distance between the subject and object. Such a project emerges from the tradition of critical pedagogy. For example, teacher educators, policy theorists, and other cultural workers concerned with democracy can devise new languages to contest the spread of consumer discourses and logic. Such democratic languages open up the possibilities for reconceptualizing social relationships in more egalitarian forms. This kind of strategy relies upon a Marxian/Freirian notion of praxis for transformation: subjects (with the help of critical agents) theorize their experience to come to a new understanding and ultimately act to change that social reality. In the Coke case a democratic language could be employed to challenge the corporation's very presence in the school, and in a broader social sense a democratic pedagogical language can challenge the market-based justifications for education that are allowing consumerism in public schools.

A reinvention of language alone is not the sufficient precondition for reconceptualizing the public schools and the public sphere. Such a struggle over language and meaning needs to be part of a broader struggle over institutional power and a fundamental transformation of existing social structures. In short, there are two major interconnected struggles to be waged: first, the struggle over the control of the means of production (the goal being the democratization of the economy) and second, the struggle over the control of the production of identities and identifications.

The economic issue of control seems to be clearer than the cultural issue at first glance. For example, we can identify a number of corporations—say, four hundred globally—that have an octopus-like hold on most of the world's wealth and resources.[26] However, the control over identification production seems elusive because identities are not only produced by a finite number of corporations such as Walt Disney but are continually constituted in daily life through interactions and nondominant institutions. For example, a gay pride parade produces identifications, as does the church, the state, the family, and so on. Nonetheless, major controllers of identification production can be identified in much the same way as major controllers of the means of material production can be identified. For example, the political economy of communications maps such concentration of cultural production in terms of mass media. The five major media conglomerates in the United States together form a major pedagogical force for identity production. Cultural theorists can map the various political, economic, and pedagogical processes that major producers of dominant cultural identifications use both to promote their products and to turn students into consuming subjects. For example, what are the major forces involved in producing capitalist cultural identifications? Such mapping work, which would coordinate work already done in cultural studies and the political economy of communications, could provide a clearer picture of how oppressive power functions and, hence, mobilize popular hope of social transformation by allowing clear identification of institutions culpable for deterring democracy. The anticorporate, propublic strategies of critical education should link the struggle against the commercialization of public schools to broader social struggles against exploitation and for democracy.

NOTES

1. The story made the "top-tier" papers such as the *New York Times, Washington Post,* and *Wall Street Journal* and was carried by the Associated Press. It also received extensive radio and television coverage. Associated Press, "Some Things Don't Go Better with Coke," *The Plain Dealer*, 26 March 1998, A16. Frank Swoboda, "Pepsi Prank Fizzles on 'Coke Day,'" *Seattle Times*, 26 March 1998, 4A. Nikhil Deogun, "Go to the Blackboard and Write 50 Times: 'Always Coca-Cola,'" *Wall Street Journal*, 26 March 1998.

2. Swoboda, "Pepsi Prank Fizzles on 'Coke Day,'" 4A.

3. Associated Press, "Some Things Don't Go Better with Coke," 16A.

4. The issue of the commercial exploitation of youth should be viewed in relation to a more general scapegoating of youth in mass media and government policy. See Mike Males's extensively researched *The Scapegoat Generation* (Monroe, Maine: Common Courage Press, 1996), which exposes popular myths about teen pregnancy, youth violence, the transmission of HIV, and welfare dependency: "Clinton and his Children's Defense Fund aides are well aware of the research showing large majorities of teen mothers suffered violent sexual and physical abuses at home, that fewer than 5 percent of under-18 mothers live in homes where no adults are present, that most 'sexually active' girls under age 15 were initiated into sex by rape by older males (often of the adult ages with whom Clinton joked about his own premarital El Camino truck-beddings), and that higher welfare payments are correlated with lower, not higher, rates of teen births," 16. The point here is the importance of viewing the victimization of youth in relation to social struggles such as the distribution of resources.

5. See Alex Molnar's comprehensive *Giving Kids the Business* (New York: Westview, 1996). On the relationship between commercialization of public education and democracy, see Henry A. Giroux, "Schools for Sale: Public Education, Corporate Culture, and the Citizen Consumer," *Educational Forum* 63 (Winter 1999): 140–149.

6. Steven Manning, "Students for Sale: How Corporations Are Buying Their Way into America's Classrooms," *The Nation* (27 September 1999): 12.

7. Manning, "Students for Sale: How Corporations Are Buying Their Way into America's Classrooms," 12.

8. Manning, "Students for Sale: How Corporations Are Buying Their Way into America's Classrooms," 15.

9. Manning, "Students for Sale: How Corporations Are Buying Their Way into America's Classrooms," 15.

10. Manning, "Students for Sale: How Corporations Are Buying Their Way into America's Classrooms," 15.

11. Henry A. Giroux, "Education Incorporated" (unpublished draft), 1998.

12. Steven Manning, "The Corporate Curriculum," *The Nation* (27 September 1999): 17.

13. Sara Eckel, "Expel Corporations from Public Schools," *Austin American-Statesman*, 6 April 1998, 9A.

14. Molnar, *Giving Kids the Business,* 7.

15. Robert Pollin, "Living Wage, Live Action," *The Nation* (23 November 1998): 15.

16. This presupposes that corporations be allowed to exist in their present state. I argue later that they should not be. Genuine democracy does not subordinate the public good to private profit of a fiscal elite.

17. Evidence to this effect can be found across the political spectrum. For example, both *Keep the Rich Off Welfare*, a left-wing book, and *Time* magazine, a publication that is both neoliberal and neoconservative in its political positions, support this claim.

18. *Time* (November 1998).

19. *Time* suggests $150 billion, but *Keep the Rich Off Welfare* offers a more comprehensive analysis that includes military-industrial debt financing and the public cost of accrued interest on corporate giveaway debt.

20. Eckel, "Expel Corporations from Public Schools," 9A.

21. Allison Berryhill, "Selling Out Our Schools," *Des Moines Register,* 12 April 1998, 4A.

22. Walter Benjamin, *Illuminations* (New York: Schocken, 1985), 223.

23. Benjamin, *Illuminations,* 223.

24. See Nietzsche's *Twilight of the Idols,* particularly the sections "The Problem of Socrates" and "Reason in Philosophy," for a very clear exposition of the denial of change, the privileging of rationality, and the denigration of instinct and the body that emerges from Platonic idealism. Contemporary French philosophers as diverse as Derrida, Deleuze, and Foucault were influenced in different ways by Nietzsche's return to a pre-Socratic (Heraclitus) embrace of change and rejection of trans-

cendentalizing thought. For example, Deleuze's claim that "there is no ideology" is really a claim that language is a force, not merely a representation of reality. Derrida's criticisms of the metaphysics of presence in *Of Grammatology* also speak to this problem.

25. Henry A. Giroux, *Schooling and the Struggle for Public Life: Critical Pedagogy in the Modern Age* (Minneapolis: University of Minnesota Press, 1988), 205.

26. See Charles Derber, *Corporation Nation* (New York: St. Martin's, 1998). In particular, see chapter 4, "Companies That Run America." "The top 200 controls the lion's share of America's economy, both directly and indirectly through their new corporate web of contractors and partners. Each of them has either assets or sales above $1 billion a year—and they account for a remarkable percentage of sales and profits in America. In 1970 manufacturing corporations with over $1 billion in assets accounted for about half of all manufacturing assets and half of all profits. By 1991, the billion-dollar giants accounted for more than two-thirds of all assets and profits," 90.

4

Collateral Damage

Military experts know that when a nation attacks, the resulting casualties are seldom restricted to the concrete blocks composing buildings. They call the human costs of organized attack collateral damage. A military euphemism, collateral damage refers to the side effects of acts of war—bodies blown to bits, bloodied shreds of human flesh, the annihilation of people. The term *collateral damage* cleanses killers of their direct responsibility for the profane renting of flesh from bone. *Collateral* means additional, auxiliary, or accompanying; secondary, or indirect. It also refers to kinship—we are all collaterally related, descended from the same bloodline. Finally, *collateral* refers to the money or property staking a loan. One must risk collateral, something valuable to lose, to benefit from making oneself indebted to someone with more. The military expression *collateral damage* relies upon the first meaning, "additional," to erase the humanity of the victims of war by suggesting that the murder of noncombatants in the name of war is a side effect of a just primary act. The term also relies upon the economic meaning of collateral to transform people into incidental costs or incidental expenses incurred in a transaction. The destruction of human life becomes a minor cost or justifiable risk incurred in pursuing the target.

The current war on public schools resonates with a broader language in other public spheres that advocates social containment over social investment. For example, the championing of the death penalty, the building of prisons, and the attack on civil rights such as habeas corpus, public gathering, and automobile passenger privacy symptomatize a growing social logic that seeks to remedy social problems by limiting rights and freedoms rather than addressing social and structural causes of social ills such as poverty, the decimation of urban social services, and growing disparities in wealth and access to institutions. This chapter examines how intensifying "law and order" logic and language playing out in mass media and policy spheres contributes to the politics of containment savaging urban, largely nonwhite schools. Central to this chapter is a consideration of the relationship between the politics of containment and its military/corporate model in public schools. I take this relationship up in particular with regard to "militarized," enforcement-minded curricula and the militarized space of urban public schools—namely, schools staffed by military personnel, schools under martial law with surveillance, police presence, metal detectors, and students in uniform. The social turn away from investing in youth and toward investing in containment suggests that in the current war on public schools it is American children who are collateral damage.

THE WAR ON PUBLIC SCHOOLS

Firmly fixed in corporate crosshairs, American public education is under fire. The current assault on public education is no longer a project solely of the right. Efforts to privatize, corporatize, and commercialize public schools with various schemes including vouchers, charter school "partnerships," in-school advertising, and corporate curricula have infiltrated the language, logic, and common sense of liberals and progressives who only a few years ago would have considered privatization unthinkable. The move to privatize public schools has to be understood as part of a larger societal shift to gut the public sphere and increasingly to privatize traditionally public institutions such as prisons, public legal defense, the medical safety net, public transportation, and national and state parks, to name a few.

Not only are such infrastructural institutions as prisons, hospitals, and schools being reduced to the logic of the bottom line, but traditionally public spaces and forums in mass media have been virtually eliminated. Newspapers, film, television, radio, and publishing are powerful forces for shaping public opinion, making common sense, and forming identity itself. Yet public control of these "public-making" technologies has become increasingly concentrated in the hands of just a few massive private conglomerates. For example, presently, all of the major TV news divisions are owned by just four companies: GE, Westinghouse, Disney, and Time Warner.[1] Of course, the increasing concentration of public space by private interests translates to intensified private pedagogies aiming to represent the concentration of wealth and power as being in the public interest. For example, news shows increasingly position viewers primarily as consumers whose chief concerns are with the low prices of commodities rather than as democratic citizens concerned with social equality and an increased standard of living for all. On CNN, Secretary of Defense William Cohen spoke of a possible U.S. bombing of Iraq in terms of the benefits to consumers at the gas pumps. The 1999 U.S.-led NATO bombing of Kosovo ("bombs for peace") was justified by President Clinton, Secretary Cohen, and Secretary of State Madeleine Albright as "humanitarian aid" and in "the national interest." This thin veneer of humanitarian sentiment explaining these caring bombs fell apart only a couple of months later. The same cast of characters explained that the United States would not intervene in Indonesia's genocidal actions in East Timor because of the United States' economic relationship with Indonesia. (It must be said that this long relationship involved the United States arming and training the Indonesian military, which committed atrocities incomparably greater than those committed by the Serbs in Kosovo.) Such incidents showcase the extent to which the logic of privatization has infiltrated the public sphere. It also highlights the dangers inherent in the privatization trend. Ethical concerns become one factor to be weighed against investments in natural resources. Social subjects are increasingly interpellated as consuming subjects; citizenship collapses into consumerism. As democracy becomes a market, democratic traditions such as the ideal of equality, the respect for human rights, and the vision of a more just future go up in smoke.

Public schools have long been a part of the democratic tradition. While tremendous work remains on rethinking the elements of a genuine democracy, this part of the public sphere continues to be instrumental in transmitting democratic values. If we are to locate a threat to the democratic ideals of a plural society, valuation of difference, and freedom, we should be looking at the aforementioned rising tide of privatization but also at the rise of right-wing extremism and other fundamentalisms. For example, fundamentalist groups such as fundamentalist Christians attempt to seize the public schools to institute a religious agenda; fiscal conservatives want the schools to become like businesses, with the bottom line dictating infrastructural demands and the dictates of the market driving the curriculum; social conservatives, such as E. D. Hirsch, see the schools as a site of struggle for the true universal values that can be transmitted through a common core curriculum.

Fundamentalists, such as the religious right and social conservatives, seek to impose their one true version of history and morality. While social conservatives argue for the inherent superiority of an already dominant, white, male, straight, European culture, the Christian right, often overlapping, spearheads an effort to Christianize this vision. Both of these fundamentalisms are strongly antipluralist. Rather than making different groups and different cultures central to national culture and to power sharing, they view difference as a threat to the one respective true vision. Hence, social conservatives call for assimilationism and the Christian right typically does not explain what happens to unrepentant Jews, gays, and others in their monologic utopia.

Fiscal conservatives are antipluralist as well. Fiscal conservatives often argue that a free market is the surest way to end racism and sexism by providing unfettered opportunities for all. This, of course, elides the histories of group oppressions that maintain and reproduce cultural and social inequalities. Excessive market freedom has proven throughout the Reagan, Bush, and Clinton years that the continuing upward redistribution of wealth has fallen hardest on nonwhites, children, and women.[2] Fiscal conservatives attempt to conflate democratic freedom and market freedom or actively oppose democracy itself as a threat to market freedom. As political theorist Nancy Fraser has pointed out, a pluralistic democracy depends upon economic justice because cultural and economic oppression are not autonomous spheres but rather are imbricated.[3] Popular self-rule and the conditions for freedom and equality demand limits on the concentration of wealth and power.

Understanding the social, economic, and political context for current educational debates provides educators and educational theorists with interpretive maps for challenging material and ideological forces that threaten the democratic tradition and hinder the possibility of democratizing all social spheres. New books and articles in education as well as mass-mediated representations of schools, students, and teachers enter into a conversation about what is to be done in the field and, hence, also propose a vision for the larger society. Academic discourse as well as mass-mediated representations often translate into policy decisions by defining and limiting the parameters of what actions become thinkable.

DISCIPLINE

Mass media and educational policy have largely responded to the aforementioned growing antipublic, antidemocratic social trends with authoritarian and antidemocratic solutions—by proposing increased enforcement of disciplinary measures. The emphasis on discipline includes tightened curricular constraints such as federally, state-, and locally mandated curriculum guidelines, and more standardized curricula geared toward the reduction of teacher autonomy, teacher deskilling, and the elimination of teaching as an intellectual endeavor. In the current climate, top-down constraints surpass even the most traditionally stifling instrumentalizing controls on teacher work. We are beyond the era of Ralph Taylor and into a whole new realm of anticritical, thought-squelching tactics. For example, some critics call for heightened top-down control in the form of the complete replacement of teacher-made lesson plans with prefabricated scripted lessons. The clearest explication of this position I have seen comes from *Washington Post* columnist William Raspberry, who sings the praises of right-wing Heritage Foundation scholars who claim that teacher creativity and thought compromises "quality."

> The most effective programs are those that require the least creativity from teachers, who must take their satisfaction not from their input but from their students' performance. . . . Some teachers are very good at improvisation; many—including most of the unsuccessful teachers—aren't. But even the best improvisers may be inappropriate for the sort of children Thad Lott [attendee at the Heritage Foundation seminar] teaches. Inner-city schools, he explains, have an unusual amount of mobility among both teachers and students. "The child who may be in three different places before finishing elementary school needs the consistency of a structured curriculum." The dilemma is that what works for students is a huge turnoff for teachers as well as for curriculum experts who are frequently seduced by "progressive" approaches: open space, ungraded primaries, whole child, whole language. Direct instruction really does sound awful. But it works.[4]

Raspberry's commentary assumes that what "works" somehow eludes considerations of the social value of its efficacy. Nazi propaganda "worked," too. Such an instrumentalist approach to schooling, which overly relies on supposedly value-free and quantifiable measures of "success," fails to account for how the successes of schooling need to be understood in relation to broader social contexts. For example, the "inner-city" (read black and working-class) student who moves three times in elementary school does so due to economic necessities imposed by an economic system none too friendly to the parents it is forcing to move and none too promising to the students contained in underresourced urban schools. Raspberry misleadingly frames the issues as a forced choice between scripted lessons versus improvisation or between teacher pleasure versus efficiency. It is no coincidence that Raspberry is an outspoken advocate of abandoning public schooling in favor of full-scale privatization. Teachers need to be critical and intellectual in order to foster critical capacities in students so that they have not only tools for survival but skills to critically engage with the conditions in which they find themselves in order to work to transform those conditions. The growth of curricular constraints, such as calls for scripting, includes the celebration of reliance upon pre-fab Internet lesson plans and the growing faith in standardized testing to enforce mandated learning.

There are high social costs of such measures: citizenship becomes defined by an anticritical following of authority, knowledge becomes mistakenly presented as value-free units to be mechanically deposited, schooling models the new social logic that emphasizes social mobility rather than social transformation—namely, it perceives society as a flawed yet unchangeable situation into which individuals should seek assimilation. The individualizing logic of this way of thinking insists that those incapable of assimilating to the way things are fail themselves. Furthermore, social differences such as class, racial, ethnic, gender, and sexual difference also become defined as "unrigorous" and perceived as a threat to the singular "rigorous" norms imposed from above.

In short, the curricular turn to discipline cannot admit the struggle over cultural values that characterizes a pluralistic democratic order. As well, the curricular turn to discipline scapegoats subject matter (such as the inclusion of nondominant histories or even, at times, the teaching of such topics as evolution) for the failures of education to offer universal quality education that does not presuppose singular, universal curricular norms. These failures, in fact, result largely from broader structural inequalities such as systemically unequal funding, as well as the concomitant corporate-led production of a culture of cynicism, despair, and hopelessness in economically devastated schools and communities.

In addition to and in conjunction with the growing emphasis on curricular enforcement, mass media and educational policy have increasingly proposed the direct coercion of physical constraint as a remedy to the problems of public schooling. This trend is exemplified in schools by the imposition of surveillance cameras, metal detectors, drug tests, solitary confinement punishments and other behaviorist control tactics, mandatory uniforms, police presence, and the hiring of military personnel as instructors and administrators at all levels of public education.

The widespread turn to discipline as the solution to the problems of public schools erases the history of how capitalist schooling has failed democracy by producing a highly unequal education system. The problems specifically facing urban public schooling are multiple and should not be understated. However, the claims to a crisis in the state of public schooling have been deliberately constructed and used by conservatives to justify market-based reform when it is precisely a market-based form of funding that has been a principal cause of the poverty of urban, rural, and nonwhite schools. The state of contemporary public schooling cannot be seen in isolation from the material and discursive histories that produced current conditions such as viciously unequal education in neighboring cities. For example, property tax–based funding of public schools and the radical de-funding of public coffers by corporations evading civic responsibility have led to what Jonathan Kozol describes as savage inequalities. The focus on discipline wrongly suggests that the problems of education stem from the failures of individuals—students, teachers, and administrators—to conform properly to a fundamentally fair system. This focus on the individual elides the structural and social conditions of public schooling. As such, the often horrifying realities of urban public schooling are viewed out of the social context that produced them. For example, several recent shootings in public schools have been portrayed in mass media as the actions of pathological white children or naturally violent black youth.[5] Seldom, if ever, are such events viewed in relation to the rising culture of despair that accompanies the gutting of social services, the economic devastation of the urban center, and the lack of adequate employment, child care, health care, housing, and other crucial public goods.

Critical educators, cultural theorists, and social philosophers have detailed a rising tide of the scapegoating of youth for social conditions not of their making. As Henry A. Giroux has noted, mass-mediated representations of urban, working-class, and nonwhite youth have functioned to scapegoat kids for the worsening conditions of urban schools. Films such as *The Substitute, 187,* and *Dangerous Minds* suggest that urban nonwhite youth define the urban space as violent and dangerous, hopeless, and beyond repair. In turn, urban white youth, in films such as *River's Edge, My Own Private Idaho, Natural Born Killers,* and *Kids,* "are framed and presented through the degrading textual registers of pathological violence, a deadening moral vacuum, and a paralyzing indifference to the present and future."[6]

> If a crisis of representation regarding youth has emerged in the 1990s, it is rooted less in a transformation of representational ideologies than in a host of complex national and global forces changing the face of the contemporary urban landscape: a downward-spiraling economy, a resurgent racism, a diminishing allocation of funds for crucial public services, the creation of Tipper Gore's Parents' Music Resource Center, and the hostile public response from many white adults to rap and urban contemporary music as it entered the mainstream. These factors, among many others, appear to register a shift from media culture's simplistic but sometimes sympathetic portrayal of youth as a lens through which to analyze the social and political dynamics at work in the larger society to its current more racist and brutalizing view. Young people are no longer seen as a symptom of a wider social dilemma—they are the problem.[7]

As cultural critics and critical educators such as Henry Giroux, bell hooks, Michael Eric Dyson, Michael Apple, and others have suggested, cultural pedagogical forces such as popular culture both produce and limit the languages people use to see, conceive, and discuss the world. A pedagogical machine such as popular culture does not merely reflect reality or merely entertain. Popular culture is in the business of educating. But popular culture does not just teach. It constructs subjectivities, forms identities, and confers or delimits in individuals a sense of agency and hope about transforming the future. By constructing both identities and identifications, popular culture, like all pedagogical forces, is an inherently political domain that contains visions for the future and constitutes the present. The representations and identifications produced by corporate conglomerates such as Disney, Time Warner, or Sony express particular conservatizing ideologies and hence often produce antidemocratic visions and identifications with positions often not in the interests of those who identify.

Those representations that define urban, working-class, and nonwhite youth as a social threat produce public consent to the introduction of new coercive measures such as the militarization of the public schools. In this sense, the struggle over representations and public meanings is as serious as the struggle over the control of bodies through the use of coercive technologies. Language and representations produce the conditions of possibility for the implementation of direct coercion, and they produce the conditions of possibility for the less direct exercise of authority through what Antonio Gramsci understood as the making of consent. Hence, in the context of an industrialized democracy such as the United States, in which power is wielded largely through the "manufacture of consent," representational politics should not be discounted as less important or secondary to direct coercion in the ways that it structures social relations in domination.

The militarization of the public schools is both a material and a cultural project. This project can be understood as a part of the rise of a "warlike mentality" in the United States that, as secretary general of Amnesty International Pierre Sane writes, is a factor in the worsening human rights record of this country.

> The human rights situation in the United States is bad, and our research shows it is getting worse. It is getting worse because there is a sort of warlike mentality in this country. There is a war on crimes, there is a war on drugs, there is a war on illegal immigrants, there is a war on terrorism. Law enforcement agencies are given a lot of scope to deal with these issues, which are presented as national threats. In a context like that, human rights are likely to be a casualty.[8]

The significance of Pierre Sane's insight rests not merely with the rising mentality of warlike thinking as the cause of an increasingly enforcement-minded education but rather with how the public conversation about social issues sets the stage and creates the context for action. The problem of education as enforcement, in part, stems from a surge in warlike thinking. However, this surge in warlike thinking is a part of a material and ideological battle waged by conservatives bent on privatizing public goods and reassigning blame for social ills to the victims from the perpetrators. For example, Johnson's war on poverty, which sought to address social inequities, becomes Reagan's, Bush's, and Clinton's war on drugs—a war on the symptoms rather than the causes of social inequities. The contemporary conservatism has a completely ahistorical and individually based law-and-order logic that pinpoints the causes of crime as criminals and the causes of poverty as the poor. This logic needs to be understood as a form of social privatization—namely, it is a privatization of social responsibility.

One of the most startling elements of the contemporary conservatism is the conjunction of nationalism, which has been rising since Reagan, with the antipublic sentiment that has also picked up speed since 1980. Common and frequent proclamations against "big government" come from across the political spectrum—conservatives and liberals as well as a growing number of libertarians and populists. Contradictorily, these conservative cries against public spending as a threat to the individual freedoms of private citizens are accompanied by insistence on extreme intervention in the private sphere: antiabortion, censorship, and increased police search and dispersal, to name a few examples. Calls to cut government spending and taxes have been used to justify decreases in social spending and the dismantling of welfare, while military spending and corporate welfare somehow elude the classifications of government spending.

Indeed, Clinton's early 1999 plans drastically to step up military spending come in the wake of his claims of having successfully trimmed big government spending. As mainstream economist Lester Thurow points out, the debt-creating tax cuts and increases in military spending under Reagan were not in fact the expression of supply-side economic theory at all but rather Keynesian welfare-state economics, in which the recipients of welfare were the military and high-tech and defense contractors. Clinton's revival of Reagan's military welfare comes with a $112 billion increase over six years, planned for the military and starting in 1999 (schools will get only $1 billion). The replacement of the Soviet threat by the terrorist threat in mass media has come to justify such flagrant corporate-military welfare. The government has been legitimating the return to near Cold War levels of military funding through a series of inventive new uses in addition to the old standby tactics. "Humanitarian aid" and the two regional conflict explanations top the list. However, attacking former allies and military aid recipients such as Iraq and Panama has not gone out of fashion. The United States defied international law and the UN in unwarranted military aggression against Iraq, Afghanistan, and Sudan at the end of 1998. One grave danger of this rising nationalism, expressed in military and corporate allocations simultaneous with the decreasing support of the public sphere, is the decrease in democratic control of the nation's international agenda.

The failures of many corporations such as EAI to profit from performance contracting or direct control of public schools has turned businesses toward other kinds of profiteering in schools. Corporate curriculum and advertising, such as KIII's Channel One, have been very successful at capturing the attention of youth to sell products. However, America's fastest growing business, the carceral industry, has provided a model for a unique new way of turning students into dollars.

Punish

Lock-down. Metal detectors, surveillance cameras, uniformed inmates, uniformed armed guards, chain-link, buzz-in security systems—countless urban schools resemble prisons. The promise of upward mobility offered by the economic efficiency justification for schooling rings true in white, suburban schools. But urban, largely nonwhite institutions do not even feign to prepare students for entree into the professional class, the class that carries out the orders of the ruling corporate-state elite. These schools contain students who have been deemed hopeless and have been consigned to institutional containment. Many urban schools function as the first level of containment while the second level, America's largest growing industry, the prison system, awaits them.

Since Reagan's mandatory drug-sentencing guidelines, incarceration rates have increased threefold, housing mostly drug offenders or perpetrators of victimless crimes. This policy targets poor and nonwhite citizens denied the opportunities of the legitimate economy. Racist drug-sentencing laws compound the carceral solution by penalizing cheaper narcotics favored by the poor, such as crack, at a rate of over ten to one. Resorting to the illicit economy makes perfect sense from the perspective of marginalized citizens, in light of the steadily declining real wage and the deindustrialization of the economy since the '70s. Given the choice of feeding a family on $5.25 an hour behind a fryolator (no benefits, no full-time hours, no overtime, no contract) or making $30,000 a week selling cocaine, the risks of dealing seem justified. This is so particularly in light of the intense corporate pedagogies of greed, selfish individualism, and Machiavellianism that have pervaded culture since the early '80s. The incarcerated are transformed into commodities in the prison industry. This effort is assisted by the cultural project of objectifying criminals on a slew of law-and-order real-life cop shows on television.

Television shows such as *Cops, America's Most Wanted,* and *America's Wildest Police Videos,* through skillful framing, fast cuts, and narrative, align the viewer with the perspective of police and military authorities. These shows create simple action movie good/bad dichotomies that always suggest the benevolence of authorities and the malevolence of a class of people called "criminals." Part of what is so disturbing about these shows is a complete lack of accountability for the often fascistic political positions espoused. For example, *Cops* routinely shows illegal police harassment and brutality in a positive light by the camera crew colluding with the sharply dressed officers who are the only ones given the opportunity to narrate their behavior, which includes police brutality, unwarranted car searches, unlawful dispersal of congregating citizens, and racist and sexist interrogations.

While *Cops* positions the viewer as on a tour given by the police, *America's Wildest Police Videos* uses actual police footage to position viewers as the police. The viewer becomes the cop chasing a suspect on the highway or the police helicopter pilot viewing his apprehension omnisciently from above. Suspects are consistently referred to as criminals despite Miranda laws or the "innocent until proven guilty" tenet of American democracy. Another disturbing aspect of these shows is the way negative representations of working-class people naturalize them as criminal, ignorant, and hopeless. Such representations remove the portrayals of working-class people from the social conditions that produce the poverty, ill health, and violence shown on the shows. The documentary style of the shows builds on a tradition of cinematic realism[9] to suggest that what is being shown is a slice of life, of the real world. This naturalizes the conditions of the subjects of the footage, rendering them eternally the way they are. Such delimitations of the subjects' history suggest an eternal present in which the individuals choose their behavior from the same conditions as the viewer. Actions then are only a matter of individual choice and character and not a matter of the social conditions that limit the range of choices available to an individual.

America's Wildest Police Videos is not only domestic. On *AWPV* the good versus evil narrative often includes footage of military troops breaking up pro-democracy demonstrations in developing nations. South Korean and Indonesian democracy demonstrators have been portrayed on the show as evil and in the wrong for battling police aggression and even for congregating in the streets. The show does not reveal anything more of the contexts than the country where the demonstrations occur. Through narrative framing and what is not shown, the situations become matters of authority and discipline versus chaos and anarchy. The law is always right on these shows because it is the law. Politics and history disappear completely, while power gets defined as good when on the side of the authorities and dangerous anywhere else, such as with people. Such cultural pedagogies form the conditions for a rising social logic of militarization and law-and-order thinking, in which the public good is redefined as alignment with the force of the law. As the attack on the public sphere grows, the law increasingly defines the public good by the corporate good. This becomes obvious as the government proposes putting social security funds into the stock market, thereby making the public good reliant upon the economic prosperity of the ruling class. Within such a social logic, public education reform looks to undemocratic models such as the military and the corporation for solutions.

Incarceration as a solution to crime has successfully distributed public funds to those citizens who need help the least—corporations building prisons and renting guards, and universities training criminologists. Crime is big business for corporations. As well, the focus on criminals as the cause of crime redirects blame from those who control capital to those suffering the most from an oppressive class system. Yet prisoners are more than commodities. They are also a form of slave labor providing subminimum wage work to airlines and other corporations that flout labor laws by using prison labor to take reservations or make products. This is not an apology for lawlessness. Rather, I am suggesting that the turn to discipline to remedy social problems disconnects those problems from the histories and conditions that produced them.

Social remedies need to emerge from a compassionate understanding of the social causes that force certain populations out of the legitimate economic circuit. However, the real reform would be to change those structures that promote exploitation, promote the transformation of people into products, and promote a cynical greed and unholy competition for banquet table crumbs. I now look more closely at the carceral solution to the problems of public schools. These solutions include the hiring of military personnel as teachers and administrators and the intensification of other martial reform in schools such as uniforms, surveillance, metal detectors, policing, and lock-ins.

Martial Law: The Installation of Soldiers in Schools

In 1996 two generals were appointed to seize command of two school districts in two Washingtons. In the District of Columbia Julius W. Becton, Jr., was described by *Education Week* as a career military man, expert in disaster relief, a great-grandfather, and titled "CEO" of the District's schools. Becton's installment followed the ousting of an elected school board by the U.S. Congress and the installation of a junta officially titled "The District of Columbia Financial Responsibility and Management Assistance Authority" and unofficially called "The Control Board." The appointment of Becton as CEO completed the "school district's new business-inspired governance structure," which was formed "to reverse the sagging fortunes of the deeply troubled school system."

> In his first week in office, Mr. Becton wasted no time in adopting "a business approach" to the district's affairs, putting employees on notice that slackers should "seek employment elsewhere."[10]

According to the paper, Becton's agenda will be topped with "combatting the violence that makes young children feel they must bring weapons to school, and correcting school building hazards that further erode their safety."

On the other coast, in the other Washington, career general John Stanton, who also has no education experience, was hired by the Seattle School District at a CEO salary level of $175,000,

> to shake up a bureaucracy handling 46,000 pupils and struggling with a 15 percent drop-out rate, constant funding shortages, painfully bad test scores and a worrying level of violence. On leaving the military he had worked as a county executive in Atlanta, Georgia.[11]

Unlike Becton's patriarchal, grandfatherly image, Stanton receives a different kind of attention.

> Seattle has learned the value of someone who, amazingly, has made the job of school superintendent sexy: He has occasionally landed at schools in a military helicopter and he has enlisted corporate sponsors from Boeing to McDonald's.[12]

A television news segment on Stanton revealed that his connections to corporations do not merely fall in his lap. They are procured with a large portion of his time spent courting private sponsorship for the public schools. Like Becton, Stanton promises a tight-fisted discipline in his schools. While Becton threatens teachers' jobs, Stanton threatens to close schools that fail to keep up with his reform plans.

Two Washingtons, two generals, both CEOs with no experience in education, promising discipline, order, and corporate structure. According to Tim Cornwell, the appointments "seem(s) to mark an increasing faith in the

military in American public life." Whether or not one were to confirm em-
pirically Cornwell's observation, this phenomenon does mark a significant
moment in contemporary educational policy and thought. However, this phenomenon cannot be understood without looking back to the entry point of war
and business metaphors in contemporary policy.

The *A Nation at Risk* report of 1983 marked the beginning of the renewed
and intensified corporate involvement in public schooling.

> If an unfriendly foreign power had attempted to impose on America the mediocre
> educational performance that exists today, we might well have viewed it as an
> act of war.[13]

The report founded a new crisis of education on the basis of a flagging U.S.
effort at global economic competition. As Alex Molnar suggests, war and global economic competition functioned to scapegoat education for the failures
of American corporations.

> The enthusiasm with which executives and their political allies responded to *A
> Nation at Risk* was not surprising. Its underlying logic cast America's enduring
> economic crisis as primarily a symptom of the failures of public education. Its
> self-assured, bombastic tone helped direct public attention away from any careful
> assessment of the extent to which the economic problems facing the United
> States were a function of structural problems in the economy, the consequences
> of deliberate corporate strategy, or a result of government policy toward busi-
> ness. It also helped create a political climate in which the pronouncements of
> business leaders assumed preeminent status in the debate over educational
> change.[14]

The culture of Reaganism, which has continued through the Bush and Clinton
eras, combined an economic and cultural attack on public education. By 1996
the idealization of enforcement, discipline, and antidependency peaked with
the dismantling of welfare, the widespread embrace of workfare, a wholesale
frenzy of antipoor sentiment, and the widespread turn to uniforms, metal detectors, and other disciplinary measures in schools. The attack on the poor
came at a time of record gains in wealth by the wealthiest segment of the
population. CEOs made billion-dollar bonuses, corporate welfare (publicly
funded handouts to corporations and wealthy individuals) totaled at least $448
billion, while welfare for the poor prior to the dismantling totaled just $71.5
billion.[15] With the collapse of the Soviet Union and no real enemies abroad,
conservatives, including retired generals and Pentagon staff, were advocating cutting Pentagon spending by an average of $155 billion.[16] Instead of

cutting what the military itself was saying it did not need, the government attacked aid to America's most needy citizens.

Generals Julius Becton and John Stanton are black. Like Gulf War general Colin Powell, they are more than success stories of minority citizens who were able to overcome the obstacles of racism to cash in on the American dream. Becton and Stanton form a narrative about difference, dependency, responsibility, and the intensifying neoliberal imperative that individuals prove their "usefulness." As disadvantaged individuals who "made it," Becton and Stanton embody the interplay between discipline and dependency. Strong individuals, they seem to have risen on their own merit and sweat. They appear as reassuring symbols to white America that opportunities are there for minorities. Ultimately, the military narrative that comes with the installment of military personnel in the schools is that the responsibility for success lies with the individual—success or failure derives strictly from discipline and self-discipline. Such a narrative covers over the extent to which social conditions such as inferior defunded schools impose limits on the range of individual agency.

Urban and largely nonwhite schools are also being targeted for military invasion in the form of retired soldiers being installed as teachers. Brainchild of the Clinton administration, the "Troops to Teachers" program was designed to provide work for retired soldiers and at the same time to provide "good role models" and disciplined instruction for children in understaffed urban public schools. The "Troops to Teachers" program is being expanded to "high poverty" schools with the placement of more than three thousand soldiers.[17] These soldiers, who mostly have no teaching experience, are benefiting from the federal government's continued pouring of cash into military welfare programs. The $18 million program has received press coverage and a proud announcement by Clinton in a State of the Union address. One must wonder why the federal government would turn to retired military personnel for staffing classrooms instead of qualified teachers, certified teachers, retired professors, or the glut of unemployed Ph.D. graduates.

Prior to the massive infusion of money into defense in the winter of 1999, the "Troops to Teachers" program was being justified by the government on the grounds that the military had been "downsized." Over the past few years more than 700,000 military personnel have been retired. However, along with the drastic increase in military funding, the "Troops to Teachers" program was expanded. This suggests that the expansion may have more to do with ideology than economics. We are informed of the ideological dimensions of the situation by listening to a principal and an instructor. Says Johnny Brashear, an elementary school principal:

He [retired soldier] comes with a level of dedication, discipline, commitment and—a sense of loyalty and duty. And I think that's a military kind of attitude.[18]

One report explains that these military instructors are far "tougher" than ordinary teachers, in terms of the amount of work assigned and the behavioral rigidity in class. We might wonder to what end exactly this discipline is enforced. Is it to make creative, free-thinking citizens engaged in shaping the social in a more democratic fashion?

An instructor in the program offers a vision that suggests otherwise:

I have a real desire and a real burning passion to help as many students as I can. I tell my students, I say: you know, I want to be able to walk into a bank one day and need a loan and need some services and see you in there.[19]

The militaristic turn has a highly assimilationist economic efficiency justification for education. Within such a view, discipline and the emphasis on strong self-discipline translate into an undemocratic form of social decision making, as the social good becomes determined by the rule of private power not of students' or most citizens' making. For example, in this case, decisions over what kind of work Americans do becomes a private decision made by a bank. Why should the kind of work and the quality of work Americans do be determined by the economic interests and capital accumulation of a few citizens rather than the interests of all workers? In the case of the previous example, the power of private industry such as banks becomes viewed as the hope of citizens in the making. Privatizing pedagogies are built in to the military reform movement.

Privatizing with Uniformity

In the past few years, many major cities have adopted mandatory uniforms for students. Cities requiring uniforms include New York, Chicago, San Antonio, Dayton, Birmingham, Oakland, Long Beach, Miami, Cleveland, and Boston. Nonurban school districts such as many in Indiana are following suit. Mandatory uniforms are being touted at a local, state, and national level as a solution to many problems of public schooling. President Clinton, in more than one State of the Union address, has claimed that uniforms will "bring order" to public schools. He subsequently ordered the Department of Education to aid school districts in strategies of uniform implementation and enforcement.

Uniforms are being attributed with the power to "bring order," make schools safer by eliminating competition over clothing, diminish peer pressure, improve discipline, promote greater school unity and pride, motivate students, enforce "civility," and unify different races and ethnicities. Newspaper articles, televisions reports, and radio exposés have largely given favorable coverage to the uniform trend. However, only one study has been conducted to evaluate the effectiveness of uniforms at achieving the previously listed goals. This, the only national study of uniforms, was funded by the Lands' End clothing company, which is one of the largest suppliers of school uniforms. That study cited improvements in school safety. An extensive recent federally funded national survey of school violence concluded that the majority of the nation's 79,000 schools *are* safe. The exceptions are "pockets of pervasive violence, mostly in larger, urban schools."[20]

Disciplinary rhetoric and disciplinary measures such as the imposition of uniforms function as capitalist pedagogy in a number of ways. First, uniforms give public schools the look and feel of private institutions. The imposition of a uniform code framed as an improvement suggests to students and parents that the private schools are the model for excellent education. As many studies have shown, on the whole, private schools do not offer better education than public schools. Yet the private school image, when adopted by public schools, promotes the idea that private schools should be the model and standard for public schools. This undermines public confidence in public institutions and suggests that private is synonymous with quality. By proffering the private school image, uniforms intensify the dangerous idea that education is a consumable commodity. This redefines citizenship as consumerism.

In addition, militaristic dress codes articulate with the rising logic of professionalism defined in managerial terms. One eighth-grade student puts it well,

> It sets the mentality in your head that you're more grown up and that you are ready for the business world.[21]

Here we see how the military imagery of uniforms contributes to a definition of public schooling along the lines of economic efficiency and the promise of upward social mobility. This idea is confirmed by President Clinton in his energetic endorsement of a reform with no evidence behind it save for a study conducted by a clothing company:

> Making them safer, more disciplined and orderly, freeing teachers to focus on teaching and students to focus on their *job of learning.*[22]

This language is not surprising, coming from an administration that brags of remaking government based on the corporate model. However, this is important for the way the focus on discipline exempts the federal government from engaging in a battle with state and local government over imposing strong authoritative federal action to equalize funding and resources nationwide. Clinton's quote points to the leveling of blame for the problems of education on badly behaving students and distracted teachers.

In light of the horrifying realities of urban education in this country, in terms of crumbling physical sites, inadequate supplies, stretched budgets, and dilapidated, government- and corporate-abandoned neighborhoods, such redistribution of blame needs to be understood as an active upward redistribution of resources, as a form of scapegoating, as racist and unethical, and as a prescription for high social costs in the long run: more crime, more disenfranchised citizenry, higher levels of cynicism and political apathy. How have the government, the mass media, and educational policy responded to a public education system besieged by the corporate sector and corporate culture?

"Uniforms are the great equalizer."[23] This quote, which comes from the business pages of the *Chicago Tribune,* reflects a widespread justification for uniform imposition. Uniforms are being positioned as democratic for overcoming fashion-conscious competition among students. Of course, the great irony here is that this divisive competition over status symbols comes from corporate pedagogies—billions of dollars in advertising teaching lessons in consumer competition, billions of hours of television watching, from films, from the Internet, and a culture of consumerism that has been sold as entertainment and that defines human worth by having consumer goods. At first glance, uniforms might seem to counter consumerist pedagogies and shallow status seeking.

"The whole point is to have the children to be equal, not to divide the haves and have nots," said Dr. Joe Haynes, superintendent of schools in Greenville, Miss., who this year expanded his district's policy to cover all students and ban all labels.[24]

However, genuine educational reform would understand public schools as one place where students can be taught to transform *a system* that divides haves from have-nots and divides whites from nonwhites. The uniform debates do not engage with fundamental questions of the role of education in transforming a system structured in divisiveness, inequality, and oppression. Furthermore, as Nadine Strossen, president of the American Civil Liberties Union, points out, the focus on uniforms is an expedient way for politicians and policymakers to create a significant change in the appearance of a school without really spending taxpayer money and without really making substantial changes in the quality of education.

Throughout society, there is popular support for any measure that sounds like it supports greater law and order, even if there's no evidence that it actually has any effect. I don't think politicians really believe in school uniforms, but they do it to get kudos, to be seen as taking action without costing the taxpayers money. And while we do get some complaints, lots of people shrug their shoulders, thinking it may not do any good, but it won't do much harm either.[25]

As well, uniform reform covers over the important social questions of how divisive capitalist pedagogies are to democratic community.

While there is no evidence to suggest that uniforms offer students or teachers benefits, there is significant evidence that in addition to appearing as a victory for politicians and superintendents, uniforms offer large corporations quite a bit.

Minneapolis-based Dayton Hudson Corp's Target division, Wal-Mart Stores Inc. and Sears, Roebuck and Co. each say that uniform sales are boosting business in their children's departments. Some doubled their uniform sales in 1996, a business that barely existed for them less than three years ago. . . . Clarence Farrar, head of operations at Goldblatt's [store] calls it a win-win situation. "The parents love it, the kids love it, the schools love it. And we love it because we love any classification that can do a million in sales."[26]

The corporate media has oftentimes produced identification with uniforms so that kids think that uniforms give them a sense of belonging when they really are creating consumer consciousness. It is hard to take seriously claims to impartiality or claims that kids love wearing uniforms from an industry estimated for 1998 to be earning $1.5 billion from uniform sales. In reality, parents are forced to invest more money in clothing and children are forced to wear the things.

The key issue around uniforms is the claim by supporters that they foster greater equality by homogenizing students' appearance. In this debate, difference is the enemy of order. Uniforms are seen by their advocates to pose a threat to difference but one that is necessary to maintain a veneer of educational reform. One ten-year-old girl sums up the positions nicely,

Public school is full of people from different races and different countries. Uniforms put us all together. It's nice to be together. It's also nice to be my own person. . . . Uniforms would not show us our unique way.[27]

What both sides of the debate fail to recognize is the extent to which identities and desires are shaped through cultural pedagogies produced and distributed by major corporations with financial and ideological interests at stake.

The uniform debates reveal a fundamental contradiction in market-based school reform. The widespread use of uniforms in public schools to protect children from competition and choice is happening simultaneously with increasing calls for school choice. This means that even as consumerism and competition are seen as saving schools (choice), they are also understood as dangerous for students (students competing over clothing). This contradiction belies the fact that the uniforms function symbolically to suggest that the problems of public schooling derive from a lack of student discipline instead of from unequal distribution of resources in schools and communities. Uniforms, like choice programs, are targeted at poor and nonwhite school districts. While choice plans suggest that the market solves all problems, uniforms suggest that the problems themselves derive not from market-driven injustices but from individual lack and cultures of pathology and deviancy. Uniforms also function symbolically by linking with racist discourses that define difference as deviance. Hence, uniforms turn issues of unequal access into discipline problems but also racialize this depiction by connecting with racist notions of nonwhites as lazy, dangerous, and in need of paternalism.

The promotion of genuine equality in schools and in society, in part, involves redistribution of decision-making power and resources from the small number of hands they are currently concentrated in to the bulk of the population. It also involves the democratization of the access to media production and the ending of commercial monopolies on the tools of meaning making. The uniform issue individualizes and limits structural concerns with genuine equality for different groups and covers over the realities of how powerful and privileged segments of society actively maintain highly unequal schooling and unequal distribution of public resources.

Critical educators and cultural workers need to reject the culture of militarization and its celebration of discipline as a dangerous ruse and a sideshow that distracts people from the possibilities for genuine democratic reform of education. As well, this rejection of militarization in public schooling should articulate with a broader public refusal to support law-and-order thinking and policy that justifies murderous U.S. policing efforts domestically and internationally. This includes rejection of a systematically racist, classist carceral system and policing, a rejection of representational violence of the sort found on cop shows, fervent opposition to U.S. terrorism in the form of bombings (Iraq, Sudan, Afghanistan), invasions, assassinations, training of death squads (School of the Americas), weapons dealing (we are by far the world's largest dealer), and assistance to oppressive regimes, as well as contestation of the economic imperialism that ultimately justifies so much of the previously listed violence. Opposition to corporate-state terror and atrocities needs to be taught in schools from a very early age. Part of the aim of this teaching should be to show the connections between consumerist and militarist pedagogies in this country and the impact and violence they cause domestically and abroad.

NOTES

1. Don Hazen and Julie Winokur, eds., *We the Media* (New York: New Press, 1997), 4.

2. See Ruth Sidel, *Keeping Women and Children Last* (New York: Penguin Books, 1996).

3. See Nancy Fraser, *Justice Interruptus: Critical Reflections on the "Post-socialist" Condition* (New York: Routledge, 1997), particularly chapters 1 and 3.

4. William Raspberry, "Sounds Bad, but It Works," *Washington Post,* 30 March 1998, 25A.

5. Mike Males, *The Scapegoat Generation* (Monroe, Maine: Common Courage Press, 1996).

6. Henry A. Giroux, *Channel Surfing: Race Talk and the Destruction of Today's Youth* (New York: St. Martin's, 1997), 44.

7. Giroux, *Channel Surfing: Race Talk and the Destruction of Today's Youth,* 44.

8. Dennis Bernstein and Larry Everest, "Cops That Maim and Kill: An Interview with Pierre Sane of Amnesty International," *Z Magazine* (January 1999): 33.

9. See Henry A. Giroux, *Fugitive Cultures: Race, Violence, and Youth* (New York: Routledge, 1996), for an excellent discussion of the political mobilization of cinematic realism in contemporary films on urban youth.

10. Caroline Hendrie, *Education Week* (4 December 1996): 6.

11. Tim Cornwell, "Military Man Takes on Problem City," *Times Literary Supplement,* 29 November 1996, 15.

12. Cornwell, "Military Man Takes on Problem City," 15.

13. Alex Molnar, *Giving Kids the Business* (Boulder: Westview, 1996), 1.

14. Molnar, *Giving Kids the Business,* 1.

15. Mark Zepezauer and Arthur Naiman, *Take the Rich Off Welfare* (Tucson: Odonian Press, 1996), 6 and 158.

16. Zepezauer and Naiman, *Take the Rich Off Welfare,* 34.

17. The placement of soldiers in schools resonates with a broader public sentiment that portrays poverty and underresourced schools as the result of a lack of student discipline. Not only does this blame youth for conditions not of their making, but it is racist in that it articulates with racist stereotypes of the lazy black and black culture as defined by deviant or pathological behavior. See Herman Gray's *Watching Race* and Robin Kelley's *Yo Mama's Disfunktional!*

18. Robert Siegel and Bill Zeeble, National Public Radio News; *All Things Considered,* 9 October 1998.

19. Siegel and Zeeble, *All Things Considered,* 9 October 1998.

20. Frank Currier, *CBS This Morning*, 20 March 1998.

21. George Lewis, *NBC News at Sunrise*, 20 March 1998.

22. George Lewis, *NBC Nightly News*, 19 March 1998 (video clip originally recorded 24 February 1996).

23. Genevieve Buck, "Retail Firms Line Up to Sell Classy Clothes as School Dress Codes Tighten, Uniforms Gain in Popularity," *Chicago Tribune*, 3 February 1997, D1.

24. Tamar Lewin, *Cleveland Plain Dealer,* 27 September 1997, 2A.

25. Lewin, *Cleveland Plain Dealer,* 2A.

26. Buck, "Retail Firms Line Up to Sell Classy Clothes as School Dress Codes Tighten, Uniforms Gain in Popularity," D1.

27. John J. Goldman, *Los Angeles Times*, 25 March 1998, 2B.

5

Pedagogues, Pedophiles, and Other Lovers: The Constructed Crisis of the Predatory Teacher

THE CRISIS OF THE PREDATORY TEACHER

Writing about molesters is easy. After all, who is going to argue that more teachers should be child molesters or that teacher education programs should screen out those disinclined to molest kids? We all know that child sex abuse is bad. Defending child molesters is a great deal more socially unacceptable than defending serial killers or even communists. This being the case, when an article appears in a major journal linking genuinely controversial educational policy issues to such obvious truths, we need to take a step back, take a deep breath, squint our eyes, and wonder what is really being argued. A recent contribution to *Educational Forum* titled "Screening Teacher Education Candidates for Sexual Predators," by Ilene and Michael Berson et al., deserves just such a healthy dose of suspicion.

The article suggests that teachers are sexually molesting children at an alarming rate and that, perhaps more important, a disproportionate number of teachers enter the profession specifically to molest children. According to the authors, this justifies drastically intensified surveillance of teachers in classrooms, more extensive psychological and character screenings, more "rigorous" teacher education programs, a weeding-out of prospective teachers who "go beyond cultural norms and expectations regarding developing relationships with minors," and FBI investigations of all preservice teachers.

In a strictly practical sense this proposal raises privacy issues, funding issues, and political issues. The cost of extensive FBI screenings runs in the neighborhood of $60,000 per teacher. If the teacher education programs foot the bill, this will radically drive up the cost of higher education, which is already prohibitively expensive for working-class and middle-class citizens. If the public schools pay, then this would drain already inadequate resources from those urban and largely nonwhite schools in need of textbooks, functional physical sites, and sufficient employees. This call for funding more discipline-minded programs to police teachers extends the current post-Littleton craze to fund increased disciplinarian tactics onto students, as is currently being done with expenditures on metal detectors, surveillance, security guards, and uniforms. With actual incidents of school violence on the decline, the transformation of schools into prisons has more to do with mass-mediated spectacles and struggles over public resources than with a rise in school violence on the part of students or teachers.

The authors warn us that we do not want to go on witch hunts for sexual predators, yet they also give us radically incorrect information as to the prevalence of sexual abuse in schools. Compare the authors' claims to the number in the editorial from which it was culled.

> Education professionals tend to be unfamiliar with the realities of abuse in school settings. Yet the problem is very real. Four states that mandated background checks of school employees found, in the first five months, more than 60,000 job applicants with criminal histories of child sexual abuse (Murphy 1992).[1]

The *Education Week* editorial by Donna Murphy actually offers a very different number.

> In four states which passed legislation mandating background checks for people applying for jobs that involve working with children, during the first five months that the laws were in effect over 6,000 job applicants were found to have criminal histories of child sexual abuse.[2]

Aside from the obvious tenfold inflation that happened in the Berson article, one must notice that the source information does not come substantiated by research, evidence, or citation, nor does it list the states in question. The Berson claim, whether intentionally doctored or printed in error, is in fact derived from another completely unsubstantiated claim. Basing their argument on spectacularly incorrect premises, the authors proceed by offering guidelines for rooting out these omnipresent molesters that raise suspicion about the most devoted, passionate, and hardworking teachers.

Locating the Origins of Predatory Behavior

I raise this issue not to attack shoddy scholarship, to defend child molesters, or to suggest that this is not a social problem. In fact, adult predation is a real threat to kids. However, we must look at a possible rise in sex abuse as a part of the broader rise in the victimization of children. As many authors such as Henry Giroux, Ruth Sidel, Jonathan Kozol, and Mike Males have pointed out, there is a war on kids in this country. The dismantling of welfare, the privatization of the remains of social services, the trying of youth as adults in criminal cases, and the growth of youth as a rich site for corporate exploitation suggests that the war on kids cannot be viewed apart from global and domestic economic and social issues.

The economic war on kids is exemplified by extensive corporate profiteering on foreign child labor, commercialization of public schools, and the end of AFDC. For example, retailers such as the Gap, Banana Republic, Disney, and Nike have been found to contract knowingly with manufacturers who exploit child labor abroad. Domestically, extensive corporate profiteering is going on in public schools in the form of corporate curricula, advertisements, and "partnerships." Youth are held a captive audience for junk food commercials on KIII's Channel One. Cola companies are securing exclusive contracts with public schools strapped for cash. School buses are selling their sides for advertising. Youth is a multibillion-dollar market for corporations that evade responsibility for the costs of funding public schooling.

The dismantling of social services and economic safety nets falls hardest on youth. Ruth Sidel points out that welfare "reform" will hurt millions of children—children, not adults, are the prime beneficiaries of these programs. As well, the dismantling and privatization of welfare has led to corporations transforming youth into commodities. How do corporations respond to the inevitable rise in "at-risk" youth that comes from the elimination of social services? Sun Trust Equities, a financial services and investment company, recently issued a report entitled "At Risk Youth . . . A Growth Industry."[3] The privatizaton of social services means that after youth have been put at risk, they can become revenue sources for massive corporations such as military contractor and for-profit welfare administrator Lockheed Martin. This raises some ethical issues, not to mention questions of the responsibilities and limits of corporations in a democracy.

The corporate exploitation of kids also involves the sexualizing of younger and younger kids in ads to sell products to adults. Calvin Klein, Benetton, and other clothing makers; magazine publishers; film producers such as Disney's Miramax, releasing films such as *Kids,* the remake of *Lolita, Clueless, Happiness, Jawbreaker,* and *Eight Millimeter;* and producers of commodified news spectacles of JonBenet Ramsey, to name a few recent examples, have been increasingly using sexualized depictions of children for profit. While I am not claiming that these images directly cause a rise in pedophilia, these images do contribute to the creation of a cultural climate in which children's bodies become objectified and defined as for adult pleasure or for adult benefit—whether for sexual titillation, economic profit, or the blame for social problems. If we are to locate a cause for the sexual exploitation of children (and I think we should), we should look to the industries responsible for objectifying children and creating the preconditions for children being thought of as plunderable; we should look to the industries that are promoting desire for kids in order to sell products. Looking strictly to teachers and the teaching profession fails to grasp where the real power lies in producing a cultural climate in which children can be abused. It also lets corporations, the single biggest exploiter of children, completely off the hook.

If we are to take this issue seriously, we must also look at how a public hysteria about child molestation is being used politically to further certain educational policy aims that go to the heart of issues of teacher work, teacher autonomy, and educational resource distribution. In short, the issue of molestation is being used to justify greater disciplinary and enforcement controls on all teachers and all students; the hysteria is used to justify changes that will affect everyone in education and to redefine educational culture.

Screening for "Cultural Normalcy"

The Berson article suggests that the best teachers are under the most suspicion.

> They are often described as highly popular or outstanding teachers. These teachers "spend a lot of time with children," often try to teach needy children, are "unusually engaging and personable," and put "students at the center of their lives" (Shakeshaft, Cohan, and Greenburg 1997, 157). Therefore, such teachers offer more time and emotional energy than most.[4]

There are a few ways to interpret this news. One, child molesters are really the best teachers and we would go out and recruit them if it weren't for that pesky molesting they do. Two, teachers who go beyond their job description because they have a passion for teaching are suspect. This second claim gets to the real issue lurking beneath the surface here. Teachers should be restricted to their job descriptions and not be allowed to have autonomy in classrooms. Decreases in teacher autonomy, teacher deskilling, standardized curricula, prefab lesson plans, scripted curricula—these are all part of removing control over teacher work from teachers. Teachers, in the authors' view, are not creative or passionate and do not go beyond the call for kids. When they do, they are abnormal, deviant, and suspect. Insisting that normal teaching practice must be restricted to the ordinary and drawing tight boundaries around teaching practice serve a very specific purpose.

Increased controls on teachers involve a cultural war on nondominant cultures. We can read this in the Berson article, which calls for increased standards to impose "cultural normalcy."

> Standards developed by the Interstate New Teacher Assessment and Support Consortium (INTASC) include dispositional dimensions that allow teacher educators to assess character elements in preservice teachers. If preservice teachers demonstrate behaviors or attitudes suggesting that they may exploit children or go beyond cultural norms and expectations regarding developing relationships with minors, then educators have a responsibility to question whether they should allow those students to complete a program that will lead to a teaching license.[5]

What culture, one might wonder, do the four authors consider normal and hence rich in "character"? In their pictures in the pages of *Educational Forum,* they look white. Two are young and married, we are told in the accompanying descriptions. They are heterosexual. As self-avowed experts on health and development, we begin to get a picture of what normalcy and good character look like. It looks white, straight, and middle class. Using the authors' ethnocentric guidelines, how can we make sense of a situation in which we have a prospective teacher from a culture such as many Arabic nations in which ebullience, warmth, and touching are a part of behavioral codes? Does this teacher become suspect? How about working-class teachers who, in the terminology of educational theorist Basil Bernstein, employ an "elaborated code" characterized by a more extensive use of the body in interpersonal communication?

What are the cultural norms and expectations regarding developing relationships with minors? If we look to the most respected members of contemporary society, the corporate elite, the CEOs, who, in the wake of *A Nation at Risk,* have been given a loud voice in educational policy-making decisions, we find that these are cultural norms for relationships with minors defined not by love and care but by systematic exploitation and profit-motivated deceit. What do the authors really mean by "screening for character"? Do they really mean screening for white middle-class affect? Does screening for "normalcy" really mean screening out homosexuals? bisexuals? people with dissenting political beliefs? The chief of police for the state of New Jersey was recently fired by the governor for saying publicly that minorities cause drug crime; the Supreme Court of the United States admits that the death penalty is racist and that nonwhites are stopped by police a disproportionate number of times, but that it does not justify changing the law. What does "character" mean in contemporary America—a land in which freedom means free markets, a nation structured in class, racial, and gender inequality? If we teacher educators are going to screen for character, perhaps we should begin our screenings in corporate boardrooms, the halls of Congress and state legislatures, or inside police cruisers.

Typically, in educational policy discourse the focus on individual character justifies a refusal to admit highly unequal social realities such as inequitable funding for largely nonwhite urban and mostly white suburban districts. The insistence on tighter character screening serves as a smoke screen for an entire system in need of character overhaul in the form of radically equalized funding and resources. I now discuss how this constructed crisis of teachers as sexual predators in fact participates in the current assault on public education and fuels the educational privatization movement.

THE POLITICAL USE OF CRISIS CLAIMS IN EDUCATION

The privatization of public schooling in the form of vouchers, charter schools, and commercialization is a part of a broader social shift in which traditionally public goods are being redefined as private goods. Education is one public entity among such goods as national and state parks, natural resources, welfare, health care, legal aid, student loans, and social security increasingly subject to the glorified call to privatize. In education, the move to privatize is often justified in mass media and policy circles with recourse to spectacular crisis metaphors to leap over the gap in evidence or rigorous argumentation that would reveal shaky grounds for undoing a long democratic tradition of universal public education. Privatization of the public schools is most commonly justified by use of market metaphors of efficiency, competition, and choice. These economic metaphors appeal to neoliberals and neoconservatives alike, in that both groups share a fiscal conservatism that places market imperatives ahead of concerns with public welfare or defines the public good as a by-product of free market ideology.

In addition to the metaphors of efficiency, competition, and choice, crisis of education metaphors are most commonly used to support fiscal conservatism by allowing a leap in logic that says that the state of public schools is so bad that the only solution radical enough would be to replace public authority and initiative with private initiative and authority. This claim garners tremendous popular support despite evidence of continual improvement in public school education and despite a mountain of evidence for the failure of past privatization experiments.[6] Crisis claims function so effectively at mobilizing public sentiment in part because they are highly illustrative and visceral. They play on emotional issues and work in a way similar to that recognized by advertising producers—by tying a product or issue to intense corporeal and sensory events through the use of evocative images, rhetoric, and framing. Sex sells, but so does fear.[7]

In general, the visceral dimension of the crisis spectacle creates a rush to judgment that stands to benefit the creator of the crisis. Crisis spectacles simplify and hyperbolize complex issues. Of course, the effectiveness of crisis cries comes at the expense of careful public deliberation, a survey of evidence, and consideration of an issue in relation to its broader social import. For example, in the case of the crisis of public education, the crisis claim effaces not only the historical data, which unequivocally counters claims for the effectiveness of privatization, but also obfuscates the issue of the damage that privatization does to education as a democratic public good.

Three of the most common of such crisis metaphors employed by public school assassins in educational policy circles and in mass media are (1) the crisis of public schools themselves; (2) the crisis of the out-of-control student; and (3) the crisis of the out-of-control teacher.[8] These three crises contribute to a construction in the popular consciousness of a public school system spinning beyond public accountability, and they contribute to a public image of the public school space as one of danger and unpredictability. In this sense, the metaphorics of crisis effectively operate precisely where the privatization argument is at its weakest. Two major failings of public school privatization are accountability and predictability. Namely—with regard to accountability: the privatization of responsibility renders a severe decrease in public oversight, a loss of public control, and unaccountability of the allocation of public funds. How much money gets skimmed by profiteers riding in limos (EAI), how honest are the expenditure numbers claimed by corporate "partners" (Whittle Communications), how much money earmarked for students finds itself in private coffers (Milken's Knowledge Universe)? Accounting and accountability become private matters as corporations use their legal status to keep numbers and decision making secret. The privatization of accountability encourages corruption and abuse.

Regarding predictability, as conservative education writer Chester Finn can attest, charter schools risk sudden closure because they lack the funding stability of public schools with strong governmental authority. The volatility of the market and the dictates of the bottom line create fickle commitments on the part of investors. If vouchers seem immune to the instability of the bottom line because of their mix of private and public elements, one should keep

in mind that the very institutionalization of vouchers redefines public education from being a universal right (guaranteed government service such as
national defense and highways) to being an *entitlement* (which brings public
schooling into the weaker and more tenuous category of welfare, social security, and other such programs). As an entitlement, public education becomes
subject to being cut as fiscal government budgets dictate. Hence, market-based
educational reform creates destabilization both through direct privatization
such as performance contracting and charter schools and through public–
private partnerships such as voucher proposals.

The issue of strong government authority and the stability of universal public education has very much to do with democratic concerns with social equality, as well as with racial and class struggle. The redefinition of education from
individual right and public good to entitlement renders poor and nonwhite
public schools most vulnerable to calls for active government defunding, based
on vague, racially coded issues such as "rigor" and "excellence"—terms that,
of course, delegitimate nondominant and ideologically oppositional knowledge, value, and culture. The first segments of the population to be hit by calls
to defund public schools would, of course, be nonwhite, working-class, and
poor—those who suffer historical deprivation of the very public services that
they stand to lose through privatization initiatives. A necessary part of the cost
of public schools is their reliability, stability, and autonomy from immediate
market conditions and investor whims. Portrayals of crises of public schools
in for-profit cultural forms such as film, television, and magazines undermine
in public discourse precisely what public schooling offers that privatized
schooling cannot—namely, security, stability, and reliability in a world increasingly destabilized by growing levels of blind faith in market principles
and in everything private.

Active media portrayals of the public school as a dangerous space contribute to the privatization effort by undermining public confidence in the advantages public schools have over privatization. In addition, the image of urban,
working-class, and nonwhite public schools as dangerous justifies their continued defunding and unequal funding as compared with their suburban coun-
terparts. Media representations of students as barbaric, uncivilized, and beyond the capacity for self-control further a conservative law-and-order logic.
The Substitute, Stand and Deliver, 187, and *Dangerous Minds* exemplify the
specter of the nonwhite and working-class student as beyond help, beyond
hope, and hence in need of an iron fist. Within this representational logic the
only recourse is a higher degree of militaristic enforcement in the form of
surveillance cameras, police, metal detectors, and uniforms. Funds that should
be spent on educational resources wind up being used to transform urban

schools into visions of prison. A market-based form of funding, which ties public schooling to property taxes, has severely defunded and destabilized urban and rural schools in the first place. It is more than ironic that market enthusiasts want to use the very same market logic that has hindered the development of truly equal public schools to solve the problems it has created. A certain meanness seems to underlie the "blame the victim" mentality that has come to shroud the funding issues surrounding public education.

As distinct from the political uses of the crisis of students found in urban nonwhite schools, in largely white suburban public schools the specter of dangerous teachers justifies antidemocratic authoritarianism in a less overt fashion than the transformation of schools into prisons. In white suburban schools, the "out-of-control teacher" justifies curricular enforcement, decreased teacher autonomy, and a higher degree of standardization and bureaucratization. As well, it justifies the continuation of an inequitable system of funding.

Public School as Dangerous Space

The crisis of the out-of-control teacher has emerged both in mass-mediated news stories and fictive narratives to supplement the crisis of the public school. The crisis of the out-of-control teacher furthers the constructed crisis of the public schools by proliferating an image of the public school as a dangerous space and hence in need of radical reform. The constructed crisis of schools varies, depending upon the geography and racial constituency of public schools. While the urban nonwhite school is rendered in mass media as a dangerous space through racialized images of violent nonwhite youth (the crisis of the out-of-control student), white suburban middle-class public schools have become represented as a dangerous space, but in a different way. In largely white suburban schools the threat becomes the predatory teacher. In order to understand the crisis of the predatory teacher, it is necessary to explain the way contradictory mass-mediated representations of youth form the basis for the constructed crisis.

As Henry Giroux has detailed in *Fugitive Cultures* and *Channel Surfing,* the scapegoating of youth in mass-mediated representations elides structural considerations that form the conditions of possibility for social ills such as poverty, illiteracy, crime, and violence. Scapegoating youth reassigns responsibility for present social realities from adults and those citizens with the most power to those with the least power to shape policy, make laws, and allocate resources. Paradoxically, the rise in the demonization of youth accompanies a rise in the discourse of childhood innocence. Disneyesque idealized childhood innocence appears in the calls for censorship to protect children from the Internet and other lucrative cultural products such as films and compact discs.

This schizophrenic stance on youth can be seen glaringly in changing legislation that, on the one hand, calls for youth to be tried as adults in capital murder cases and, on the other, calls for censorship and increased prohibitions on the distribution of birth control and abortion information and services for those under eighteen. As youth are increasingly demonized and scapegoated for social problems, they are at the same time infantilized through patronizing policies and ethically, politically, and intellectually bankrupt cultural products. Such cultural products actively prevent youth from taking social responsibility and social action by limiting the range of social identifications to those ideologically consistent with highly individualized consumer identities.

The ideal of childhood innocence found in mass-marketed cultural products stands starkly at odds with the practices and politics of these cultural producers. For a very obvious example, Disney, which has built an empire on idealized childhood innocence (Magic Kingdom, Cinderella, Bambi), owns ABC TV and ABC Network News, which thrive on sensational, tabloid-style, lurid news accounts of dangerous youth (this includes *Nightline, 20/20,* and *Prime Time Live*).[9] Furthermore, Disney, producer of *Bambi, The Little Mermaid,* and *Cinderella,* also owns Miramax, Hollywood Pictures, and Touchstone, which have produced *Pulp Fiction,* Larry Clarke's *Kids,* and other films representing youth as social threat, particularly in the school setting.

My point here is not to call an alarm about negative representations of youth in media or to suggest that youth are not innocent and not in need of protection. Rather, my concern is with how claims about the innocence and culpability of youth are used by cultural producers with a disproportionate amount of public voice to remake public discourse, remake common sense, and justify social policies that benefit these corporations at the expense of kids and teachers. In short, such cultural representations reassign blame for social ills to the victims of the corporate-led assault on the public sphere. One of the ways this reassignment of blame is accomplished is though the creation and publication of narrative accounts that position children as innocent victims of uncontrollable educators.

While I have discussed the constructed crisis of education and its political uses and the crisis cries of the out-of-control student, I would now like to discuss the crisis of the out-of-control teacher and the unique ways that it contributes to antidemocratic privatization efforts.

The panic about the out-of-control teacher depends upon the mass-produced ideal of childhood innocence. Yet this notion of childhood innocence is highly race and class specific. The image of the predatory teacher differs from other simultaneous representations of teachers found in popular cultural products. Popular films such as *187, Dangerous Minds,* and *The Substitute* and its sequel represent teachers in urban settings as unstable and at the end of their ropes, burned out, or homicidally vengeful toward volatile populations of uncontrollable nonwhite students. Suburban teachers appear less as commandos and frazzled burnouts and more like bumbling incompetents in films such as *Ferris Bueller's Day Off,* other John Hughes films of the '80s and '90s, or *Clueless.* However, the out-of-control teacher as predator image—the pedagogue who preys upon youth—can be located with the highly publicized case of suburban Seattle school teacher Mary Kay Letourneau's conviction for rape following a four-year affair with her male student.

Mary Kay Letourneau and the Specter of the Predatory Teacher

In February of 1998 Seattle-area school teacher, wife, and mother Mary Kay Letourneau was arrested for talking in a car with her fourteen-year-old lover and former student. She was charged with breaching her probation from a 1996 conviction for the then-recent sexual aspects of a relationship that began as a friendship and mentorship six years earlier. Following her initial conviction, her probation required her to attend sex offender counseling, take medication for the mental illness alleged to have caused her love, and avoid all contact with her lover. Having already given birth to a girl by her lover, Letourneau was sent back to prison pregnant with his second child to complete a seven-and-a-half-year sentence for child rape. The cover of *People* magazine screamed, "Out of Control."[10] The sensational case received international notoriety.

In France, where the case garnered much attention, a book highly sympathetic to Letourneau was published, entitled *Le crime de l'amour* (*Crime of Love*). This book suggests that Letourneau and her Samoan-American lover are the victims of a cruel puritanical moralism that cannot admit the possibility of love between partners of such a great age difference when the woman is the older party. In the United States Letourneau has received very little sympathy or support from the media and the courts. While prosecutors characterize her as a child rapist, her own legal defense has characterized her as suffering from a psychological medical disorder that they admit as irrational and pathological behavior. "She was fixated on this one boy, and she had been under a no-contact order. . . . It just underscores how deep-rooted this compulsion is."[11] Newspaper and television reports of the events borrow from the perspectives of the prosecution and defense to weave together a picture of Letourneau as both a sexual predator and psychologically deranged. It is taken for granted in both the courts and the mass media that the actions of Letourneau are not only illegal and immoral but also irrational. It has also been assumed that her actions are equivalent to those of a male child rapist. Letourneau herself, however, argued at the original sentencing that the relationship was "natural, romantic love." Her lover has maintained the same, and he has insisted that he initiated the sex. His mother also supports the relationship, arguing that the two genuinely love each other.

On the most cursory level the mass media produced a narrative in which a teacher imbued with the public trust broke that public trust because she followed her irrational bodily instincts—she was a sexual predator or madness rendered her incapable of rationality. The two explanations amount to the same claim: a dangerous loss of rationality that threatened youth. The only argument is over where the agency resides. If Letourneau really loves and desires the boy, then she irrationally decides to give in to her desires. In this case, the giving-in renders her an active agent culpable for her actions. In this case, her love is real but selfish because she pursues it despite the "damage to the child." In this instance, her irrationality derives from her failure to contain her desire and conceal her love by mastering herself. The only rational recourse to such failure of self-control is to put Letourneau in prison to protect her lover from her. This, despite his insistence and his family's that the relationship is consensual and loving and despite the assurances of psychological experts that no damage seems to have come to the boy as a result of the relationship. On the other hand, if the defense attorneys are correct, then Letourneau's love for the boy is a sickness, a mental malady for which she is not responsible and from which she can be cured. She is the victim of "bipolar" disorder, a form of manic depression, it is said. In this case, Letourneau's love, though experienced by her, is *inauthentic* because it is produced by a disease. With the proper medicines and discussions with expert therapists, Letourneau can be brought to the rational position of not loving her lover and the father of two of her children.

These supposedly rational solutions by the state to what has been identified as a problem and social threat seem highly irrational. However, perhaps the claims to Letourneau's irrationality are flimsiest in light of the very Western idea of "falling in love"—an idea upon which Letourneau's story depends. Classic literature as well as popular magazines such as *People* and *Cosmopolitan* and blockbuster films such as *Titanic* rely upon this idea of "falling in love"—of the wonderfully sudden loss of rationality that accompanies an unlikely encounter between people. The more unlikely and irrational the pairing in a sudden romance, the greater the romantic proportions assumed. Falling in love demolishes sensibility but also spans seemingly unbridgeable difference. For example, in the film *Titanic,* the heroine Rose aspires to sensible, ruling-class marriage with its rational and secure financial future. Rose, of course, falls in love with Leonardo DiCaprio's romantically free, working-class artist character, Jack, who embraces chance and fate and eschews security and capital. The Falling in Love story really *is* about falling, falling from the elevated heights of rationality and the safety of social approval and the security of capital. In fact, this is literalized in *Titanic.* They meet with him trying to save her from falling off the ship, an enterprise in which he succeeds temporarily, only, of course, to fail in the end. The falling in love story is, in a sense, a letting go, a freedom from social constraints, and usually, hence, a formula for disaster. Letourneau's tale is the stuff of classic romance: true love, against all odds, overcoming the disapproval of the laws of the state and the family and the church. Yes, love is irrational, and Letourneau's love defies sensibility. Letourneau, however, has become a public monster and unlike Rose in *Titanic* her romantic irrationality has been defined as a threat and pathology rather than something to bask in. Why might this be the case?

We know how these stories go even before we open the book or the *People* magazine or enter the theater. The falling in love story is also almost always a morality tale with a pretty heavy moral. Mary Kay Letourneau poses a threat to the social order by transgressing the tightly drawn bounds of her assigned identity as a teacher, a woman, and a member of the professional class. Her uncontrolled and uncontrollable desire poses a threat to the social order in terms of class and gender relations. Popular scorn and media spectacle derived not merely from the fact that Letourneau broke up a nuclear family or left her family for a lover. In the Letourneau case an older narrative of the evil predatory mother merges with the more recent yet intensifying narrative of the predatory female teacher.

PRIVATIZATION IS A FAMILY AFFAIR

The evil-mother narrative takes different forms. The end of 1998 saw a shot-by-shot remake of *Psycho,* a tale of pathology born of consuming, overbearing, and colonizing motherly love. The horror and science fiction traditions are infused with the evil predatory mother coming to consume/get you, breeding all over you; the absent mother whose absence drives the malevolence; or the mother who produces mutants. *Alien* and its three sequels, *The Exorcist, The Brood, Invasion of the Body Snatchers, The Hunger, Carrie, The Omen* (lack of authentic good mother), *Close Encounters of the Third Kind, Dead Ringers, Videodrome, The Thing, Starship Troopers,* and *Independence Day* are a few examples of this tradition, which are almost always tied up with other narratives stressing the horrors of invasion by some predatory social force: communism (*Body Snatchers*), immigration (*Independence Day*), homosexuality (*Psycho*), the state (*Total Recall*), or urban nonwhites (*Blade Runner*). In these film traditions, the social threat takes the form of the uncontrollable mother. If the previously mentioned falling in love stories are about spanning unbridgeable difference, then the horror and sci-fi traditions are about the threat of difference. In almost all of these films, the mother gives birth to the social threat of difference. She is the line between order and disorder. It is she who allows the passage of social threat into the safe spaces that secure the social.

Aside from the home, the school and the church are the safe places of the cinematic world. Horror often depends upon the spilling-over of threat into these bastions of family values. Almost every slasher film involves the invasion of the home (usually while the parents are away and a baby-sitter is there) or the summer camp—the places where kids are out of parental watch. In Hitchcock's *The Birds,* the school provides refuge from the attacking scourge. Horror builds as the monster beaks appear through cracks they have made in the school walls. In the '80s film *Red Dawn* the communists invade, parachuting right into the schoolyard of the American heartland. In *The Sweet Hereafter* the horror of chance is produced by a yellow school bus of children careening off an icy cliff and into a frozen lake. The specter of the out-of-control teacher derives in part from the spectacle of the safe place of school invaded by danger. The recent onslaught of news stories about school violence, despite no actual rise in school violence rates, has mobilized frenzied calls for emergency actions and a lot of finger pointing to assign blame rapidly. As well, hate-mongers are given voice in mass media to suggest that homosexuals are a predatory threat to children in educational settings. According to Jerry Falwell of the Moral Majority (sic) the Teletubby with the lavender triangle is teaching your kid to be gay. The Mary Kay Letourneau case resonates with these other spectacles by allowing fingers to be pointed at female teachers as *the* problem. This reassigns blame from the issues of social responsibility for the health of public education to the female teacher as failing parents and threatening youth by infecting the safe space of school with deviance, pathology, and dysfunctionality.

Representations of the invaded school simultaneously suggest that the school is endangered by "dysfunctionality" and suggest that the school is a wholesome place, that the school is "functional." Representations of the invaded home commit the same kind of double suggestion, in which the positioning of the family as threatened by dysfunctionality simultaneously portrays the home in an idealized fashion as a wholesome and functional place. This *Leave It to Beaver* idealization of the family (of course, this is the heterosexual nuclear family) denies the fact that due to social and economic conditions the American family *is* "dysfunctionality"—emotional and physical abuse, domestic violence, sexual predation, incest. It is a tiny fraction of American families that are not defined by one or many of these "pathologies."

In fact, economic constraints play an enormous role in producing broken nuclear families and undermining whole ones. For example, the need for two earners produces the latchkey child. As well, the instability of the economy uproots middle-class families with the necessity of geographic transiency. For working-class families for whom moving is not an option, the post-Fordist departure of work intensifies familial tensions by creating economic desperation, uncertainty, and the loss of job security and health care. Narratives of familial pathology displace the realities of economic desperation. The cultural assignment of deviance to groups such as nonwhites, homosexuals, and immigrants as a threat to family values hides the reality that capitalism (along with the racism, classism, and homophobia that it produces) is the greatest threat to family values.

The portrayal of the threatened family paints a distorted idealized picture of the normative family defined by heterosexuality, whiteness, spooky sterility and innocence, and impossible, prescribed normalcy. More than this, though, the representation of the threatened family operates in American mass media to center the family as *the* social unit. The centering of the family renders it the locus of agency and responsibility.

This centering of the family and marginalizing of the social privatizes social responsibility by suggesting that social problems such as poverty or crime result from bad parenting rather than from social and structural causes such as a lack of available jobs, lack of a social safety net, or a culture of desperation and hopelessness brought on by systematic economic and cultural exclusion.

Likewise, representations of the invaded school simultaneously paint an impossibly romantic, nostalgic Norman Rockwell portrait of the school as the wholesome space it never was, while showing it under siege by the deviant forces of pathology. The threat to freedom posed by communists falling out of the sky into the schoolyard suggests that schooling prior to the landing was all about freedom. The fact is, public schooling, for all its virtues as a public good and as necessary as it is to provide universal education, has a history steeped in classism, racism, capitalist propaganda, sexism, and indoctrination into dominant ideological positions. The lived experience of public schooling is marked by oppression, domination, but also resistance on the part of both students and teachers. The school is a complex and contradictory ideological terrain. Representations of schools under siege function largely to conceal this fact. This concealment translates into political uses such as the blaming of urban and nonwhite schools for lacking the wholesomeness idealized in representations of crisis. This denigration functions to justify the continued unequal system of allocation of resources. It also exculpates those assigned representational wholesomeness—namely, wealthy people, white people, heterosexuals, and suburbanites. As well, this functions to insist upon the centrality and superiority of curricula reflecting these groups' interests. The Mary Kay Letourneau story forms the locus where the "crisis" of the pathological home and the "crisis" of the pathological school converge to hide the real causes of gross inequalities in schools and society and to hide the inequities in the distribution of public funding.

The constructed crisis of the out-of-control teacher appears not only in educational policy discourse and in print media but in popular film as well. The late 1998 science fiction film *The Faculty* offered a complex commentary on the crisis of the public schools and the crisis of the out-of-control teacher. *The Faculty* tells the story of an alien invasion of an Ohio high school. As the teachers are rapidly taken over by the aliens, a small group of students leads the resistance. The film opens with teachers at the mostly white high school discussing the funding shortages hindering their performance. The principal tells her teachers that they had better improvise and make do with their inadequate resources. When the drama instructor asks the principal how she can put on a performance of *Guys and Dolls* without money for a set, the principal callously tells her to use the set from last year's play, *Our Town,* a play with no set. Funding shortages in the film remain confined to local and community causes. There is no sense of neighboring communities competing for funds or of impoverished urban or rural areas being denied adequate funds.

The invading parasites promise harmony, the erasure of social conflict, the overcoming of difference, in short, a utopian social egalitarianism resembling the promise of communist ideals. In *The Faculty* the great danger posed by the communistic aliens is the loss of individuality that accompanies colonization. Individual difference is lost as one's own interests become intertwined with those of the community.

In the case of both Mary Kay Letourneau and *The Faculty* teachers are bodies out of control: they become the locus of irrationality defined by the loss of rational autonomous agency. Like the Letourneau story, *The Faculty* actually stages a scene of teacher seduction. Prior to colonization, Zeke, the burnout drug dealer, unsuccessfully attempts to seduce his schoolmarmish teacher in a none too subtle manner by offering her condoms. After being colonized by the alien, this same teacher becomes a seductress. She transforms in appearance—glasses are gone, hair comes down—and she tries to kiss Zeke. He resists her attempts, knowing that she wants desperately to infect him with the parasite. As in the Letourneau case, the loss of autonomous rationality results in the loss of female teachers' abilities to master their desire and their own bodies. This loss of female rationality involved in seduction appears in both narratives to threaten youth. In *The Faculty* the out-of-control teacher offers the seduction not only of sex but of a utopian social ideal. The film uses the "inappropriateness" of sex between teacher and student to place a negative moral judgment on challenges to patriarchy. Is not the same true of Letourneau, who sought to evade the strictures of the patriarchal nuclear family? In both cases female sexual control signifies a horrifying overturning of hierarchies.

This portrayal of dangerous female teachers as irrational, uncontrolled, libidinous creatures becomes literalized in the kiss scene. As the teacher relentlessly pursues Zeke, he attempts to escape by running her over. She is beheaded in the crash. Yet within moments, her body still attempts to pursue her prey, and her head scurries over to reconnect at the neck. The seducing teacher literally loses her head in her attempts at seducing her student.

Such a claim of the dangerous loss of rationality of the libidinous female teacher functions to reinforce a notion of teachers as ideally rationally directed talking heads, espousing disembodied objective truth, and removing subjectivity from the teaching process. Female sexuality represents the school's uncontrollability, effacing the problem of funding addressed initially in the film. A discourse of feminine danger comes to replace the possibilities of social critique or public policy debates. As in the Mary Kay Letourneau story, a representation of the unstable public school merges with the narrative about broken homes, which is about private failures rather than about the corporate invasion and control of public spheres.

Teachers and other cultural workers need to resist the tentacular hold the corporate sector is exerting on all aspects of contemporary society. In part, this means critically engaging with the multiple ways that popular culture functions pedagogically to spin dominant discourses. More specifically in this case, this means rejecting the constructed crises of public schooling, rejecting market language and market-based justifications for educational policy, and looking to the democratic feminist and critical traditions for ethical and political referents to guide teaching practice. As well, this means linking pedagogical practice to political struggle and linking public schooling as a vital public good to broader struggles for social transformation toward economic and cultural equality and justice.

NOTES

1. Ilene R. Berson, Michael J. Berson, Linda Karges-Bone, and Jonathon K. Parker, "Screening Teacher Education Candidates for Sexual Predators," *The Educational Forum* 63 (1999): 150–155.

2. D. Murphy, "A Scandalous Issue: Mass. Catholic Diocese Settles Suit Over Child-Abuse Charges," *Education Week* 12, no. 15 (1992): 25–26.

3. William D. Ryan, "The New Landscapes for Nonprofits," *Harvard Business Review* (January/February 1999): 129.

4. Berson et al., "Screening Teacher Education Candidates for Sexual Predators," 151.

5. Berson et al., "Screening Teacher Education Candidates for Sexual Predators," 152–153.

6. For a discussion of the constructed crisis of public education despite empirical evidence of improved quality, see David Berliner, *The Manufactured Crisis* (New York: Longman, 1995). See also Jeffrey R. Henig, *Rethinking School Choice: Limits of the Market Metaphor* (Princeton: Princeton University Press, 1994).

7. This is not an assertion that the body and emotions are bad, dangerous, and irrational as distinguished from disembodied cognition. Rather, people need to take seriously how the body is so effectively used ideologically to justify policies and political positions.

8. For a discussion of some dangers of the "bad news" education reporting bias, see Laurence Ogle and Patricia Dabbs, "Good News, Bad News: Does Media Coverage of the Schools Promote Scattershot Remedies?" *Education Week* (13 March 1996): 46. For an extensive discussion of the growing onslaught of "dangerous youth" representations, as well as the implications for education and democracy, see Henry A. Giroux, *Channel Surfing: Race Talk and the Destruction of Today's Youth* (New York: St. Martin's, 1997) and Henry A. Giroux, *Fugitive Cultures: Race, Violence, and Youth* (New York: Routledge, 1996). For a good introduction to the way crisis sells, see Murray Edelman, *Constructing the Political Spectacle* (Chicago: University of Chicago Press, 1988).

9. For a detailed account of the politics of youth representations, see Henry A. Giroux's *Channel Surfing* and *Fugitive Cultures*.

10. Bill Hewitt, Lorenzo Benet, Johnny Dodd, Leslie Berestein, Elizabeth Leonar, Elizabeth Reno, "Out of Control," *People* (30 March 1998): 44–49.

11. Associated Press, "Former Teacher Is Caught in Car with Boy Whose Baby She Bore," *Portland Oregonian,* 4 February 1998, 1B.

Conclusion

Public education is inherently political in that public schools are places where citizens are made and particular visions of democracy are propagated. The questions that educators and other cultural workers need to ask are, "What kind of citizens do we want to make?" and "What kind of democracy do we want to have?" The history of public schooling in America is rife with highly undemocratic traditions such as racism, sexism, and classism; adherence to cultural canons at odds with difference; and the blind support of state institutions that have failed in many regards to live up to their theoretically democratic commitments. As well, the continuing inequities structured into public education, such as the funding system, form the basis for many advocates of privatization to claim that it is time the public give up on public schooling. In fact, the question of public support for public education gets to the heart of contemporary struggles over the meaning of democracy. Are we to go along with the current trend to privatize everything and to annihilate the public sphere? Will democracy become merely a synonym for capitalism? I have shown in all of the preceding chapters the dangers such a vision poses not only for America's public schools but for American society more generally: the concentration of power, control, agenda setting, and decision making in the hands of a ruling economic elite; the dangerous deepening of an apartheid-like state, pitting white against nonwhite and urban against suburban; the growth of a quasi-fascist cultural logic of discipline and enforcement rather than investment in human potential and the deepening of a critical and democratic consciousness; the redefinition of human identity—social subjects turned into consuming subjects—in a way that renders critical consciousness and democratic transformative vision obsolete.

The historical failures of public schooling and the crisis of democracy do not form the basis for retreating from public education, turning our backs on it, or handing it over to deep pockets. On the contrary, the current crises of public education and democracy itself demand now, more than ever, a recognition of the power public schools have as a site of struggle for public education as a route to a deeper and more meaningful democracy. It is imperative that past failures of public education, such as the failure to properly invest in it, form the basis for a renewed effort to transform a cynical politics of containment in the urban space (in the wake of the Littleton spectacle everywhere), and transform the increasingly lottery-like politics of upward social mobility into a democratic politics that invests in youth as shapers of a more just, equal, and fair future in all social spheres.

Central to the current crisis is the fact that now, unlike any prior time in educational or even American history, the very notion of the public good is under siege. Educators must take the burden upon themselves to be attentive to how capitalist schooling and capitalism more generally are undermining schooling as a public sphere. Conscientious educators need a new language to renew and rejuvenate a strong sense of the public good. Teachers and other cultural workers need to draw on democratic traditions in order not simply to recover a strong sense of the public good but to infuse it with some of the more liberated and critical insights the present has to offer. The vibrancy of contemporary academic discourses such as the more critical variants of cultural studies, the political economy of communications, postcolonial theory, feminism, multiculturalism, and critical pedagogy offer exciting possibilities for rethinking a renewed and more radically democratic sense of the public good. These discourses have the potential to provide educators with the tools to rethink contemporary democracy in ways that will expand economic and cultural justice.

Educators and cultural workers also have open to them the possibilities of rethinking their role as professionals. Teachers need to recognize their role as public intellectuals. In this sense, teachers are not merely in the business of passing on knowledge but understand the significance of their practices as fostering particular social visions. By critically engaging students and curricula with regard to issues of power and politics, teachers, by virtue of their location, have tremendous potential to counter "publicity intellectuals" in mass media who advocate oppressive and hierarchical social relations as well as unquestioned knowledge and authority. Teachers can draw on the previously mentioned academic discourses to foster and hone their critical capacities. The role of teachers as critical public intellectuals needs to be understood as a central component of democratic education.

A renewed public language and the rise of the teacher as public intellectual are necessary yet insufficient prerequisites for the struggle for the public sphere and critical public education as a part of that struggle. Teachers need to connect their struggles and practices to the vibrant and prolific array of contemporary social movements. While most of us do not think of the present "new guilded age of capitalism" characterizing the '90s as a time of activism, according to Noam Chomsky we are witnessing a greater popular involvement in activism than in the '60s. Charles Derber offers four useful categories of contemporary social movements that are struggling against corporate power and struggling for human and social values. Educators fighting for a renewed democratic public sphere and public schools already share common struggles with the labor movement, the "third sector" of grassroots community groups, populist multiculturalists, and green populists.[1] While the current threats posed by an unbridled capitalism are dire indeed, perhaps never before have the possibilities for multiple social movements to link up seemed so promising. For example, educators share with those in the labor struggle an interest in struggling against workplace exploitation domestically and abroad. Likewise, social movements struggling for racial equality are especially pertinent to educators teaching to transform the racist institutions that they inhabit. Of course, what all of these movements share is a strong belief in nonmarket public values and the dream of a renewed democracy that is defined not by the logic of the bottom line but instead by the realization of the best elements of the democratic, socialist, feminist, postmodern, and humanist traditions.

NOTE

1. See Charles Derber, *Corporation Nation* (New York: St. Martin's, 1998). In particular, see chapter 15, "The Four Movements to Join."

Index

About the Author

Kenneth J. Saltman is an assistant professor in the Social and Cultural Studies in Education Program at DePaul University.